OIL FIELD CHILD

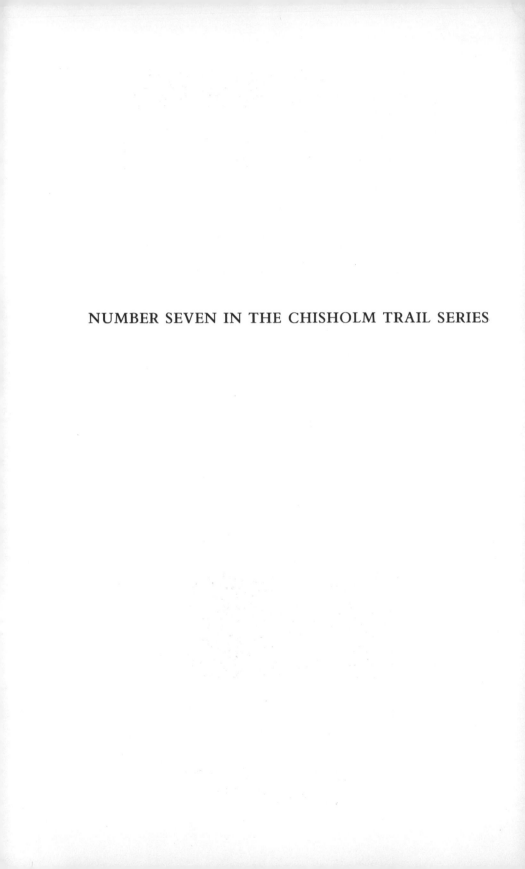

NUMBER SEVEN IN THE CHISHOLM TRAIL SERIES

OIL FIELD
CHILD

by Estha Briscoe Stowe

Texas Christian University Press
Fort Worth

LIBRARY OF CONGRESS
Library of Congress Cataloging-in-Publication Data

Stowe, Estha B. (Estha Briscoe), 1916–
    Oil Field child / by Estha B Stowe.
        p.   cm. — (Chisholm trail series ; no. 7)
            ISBN 0-87565-033-3
    1. Stowe, Estha B. (Estha Briscoe), 1916–   —Childhood and youth.
2. Texas—Biography.   3. Oklahoma—Biography.   4. Petroleum industry
and trade—Texas—History—20th century.   5. Petroleum industry and
trade—Oklahoma—History—20th century.   6. Texas—Social life and
customs.   7. Oklahoma—Social life and customs.   I. Title.   II. Series.
        CT275.S8766A3   1989   88-20141
        976.4'06'0924—dc19   CIP
                [B]

Contents

Foreword

TO A GREATER DEGREE than may be generally realized, the oil field boomtowns of Texas and neighboring states were an extension of frontier-era boomtowns that sprouted up after the discovery of gold and silver in much of the West. Oil, after all, was another mineral. Like the others, it offered employment as a solid lure and the hope of quick riches as an additional inducement for those who sought Fortune's smile.

Just as the core of the earlier mineral boomtowns was the pick-and-shovel miner, the core of the oil field rushes was the working man—the roughneck, the driller, the pipeliner, the derrick builder, the muleskinner and truckdriver. With them came all those in the necessary service industries—the storekeeper, the cafe operator, the hotelman, the mechanic. And swarming in their wake was another group, of questionable necessity but no less inevitable—the gambler, the bootlegger, the prostitute, the highjacker.

In most accounts of the oil booms, these elements have received more attention than the man who was just out there doing his job day by day, working like a mule, living more often than not under conditions little less primitive than those of his forebears in the gold and silver towns of the Old West. Often he stood in line to get even the poorest kind of meal in an overcrowded boomtown hash house. He was lucky to have any kind of roof over his head at night, even one of canvas. If single, he might sleep by shifts in a flophouse where some tired roughneck just off "tower" was waiting for him to relinquish his cot. As one oilfield veteran put it, the food was usually cold and the bed usually warm.

Much of the literature and folklore of the oil fields pays little notice to the fact that many of these workers had families who tagged along with them as they moved from one developing field to another through Oklahoma and Texas and New Mexico. Stories of boomtown violence and spectacular oil field disasters are numerous, but not a lot has been written about how families survived and often even thrived in the hurly-burly and uncertainty of the oil patch.

Estha Stowe's recollections of the oil field life as she saw it in her girlhood give another dimension to the boomtown epic. Today's reader may be appalled at the hardships which these oil field women and children endured so the working man's family could be held together. Yet, it is evident that neither Mrs. Stowe nor her mother regarded them at the time as being all that bad, or even out of the ordinary. Most of the people they knew were living through the same experiences.

Though it is probable that a certain amount of violence was going on around them, Mrs. Stowe does not dwell upon it and indeed as a girl was probably not even particularly aware of it. Children were usually sheltered from that side of boomtown life as much as possible. A telling incident is the one in which she and her friend Jewel, living briefly in McCamey, were counseled not to approach the rooming house that had three red light bulbs glowing in the night. They had no idea what kind of activity was going on there.

That oil field work could be highly dangerous was brought home to her at least twice: once when her father almost succumbed to fumes while gauging an oil tank, and again when her friend Mr. McDonald was blown to pieces in the explosion of a boiler.

From the standpoint of a child, possibly the greatest hardship of oil field life was not the primitive living conditions but rather the frequent necessity of packing up and moving to a new town, a new field, leaving old friends behind and having to cultivate new friends from among all those strange faces at the next landing place. Among the saddest experiences in Mrs. Stowe's book are these partings, and the happiest are occasional unexpected reunions with old friends in a new surrounding.

Having spent my boyhood in an oil patch environment, I can relate to Mrs. Stowe's account. I grew up on a ranch nine miles from Crane, one of the boomtowns in which she lived for a brief period shortly before my family moved there. The children with whom I went to school were products of the oil fields. Our family stayed put, but many of the others did not. Like Mrs. Stowe, I frequently found myself saying goodbye to friends whose fathers were moving away to work in other fields. I was constantly trying to become acquainted with new kids introduced into class. Sometimes I barely got to know their names before they were gone again. The oil patch in those days had a highly mobile population.

Crane as I first remember it was still much as she describes it and other towns of its kind, born of oil discovery and living for the moment because oil booms had a notoriously short existence. Few buildings in the town had been constructed with any view toward permanence. The trailer house or mobile home as we know it today was still in its infancy and did not come into general use in oil field towns for another decade or more. Many people lived in simple "shotgun" houses, quickly and cheaply constructed, given that name because they were usually long and narrow, one room leading to the next without any hallways. It was said you could fire a shotgun blast through the front screen and it would go out the back door.

Many people lived in tents, some partially boarded up inside for better protection from the weather, some not. Crane was often described as a "ragtown" in its early years, a derisive name that clung to other boomtowns of the period.

I remember being invited to look into one family's "mobile

home," an old bus that had been converted into crude living quarters. It seemed to me, as a boy, that they had neatly solved the problem of frequent moves from one oil field to another. Not until I was older did the full impact of their privations finally soak in on me.

Her accounts of early transportation problems struck home. The Crane County sandhills were deadly for early automobiles and trucks. Many an engine was burned up trying to free a vehicle entrapped to the hubs. Until they disappeared in the scrap-iron drives of World War II, old rusted hulks were scattered over the sandier parts of the ranch, abandoned where they had died before the oil companies and the county finally began to build usable caliche and oil-topped roads.

For a time Crane had no municipal water system. Many residents bought drinking water by the barrel out of a truck that brought it from a good sweet-water well a few miles from town. They kept the barrels covered with canvas or boards, and it was a minor calamity when a wandering cow, horse or burro worried the top off of a barrel and helped itself to the water.

Mrs. Stowe tells about her father working on the historic original Santa Rita No. 1 well which had started the Permian Basin oil boom in 1923. A veritable forest of derricks grew up around that well in the years that followed. Much of it still stood into the 1950s. Gradually the tall derricks were dismantled and unobtrusive pumpjacks put in their places. The only derrick still standing in the giant field that Mrs. Stowe knew near old Texon is on the site of Santa Rita No. 1, and it remains only as a memorial. Even that derrick is of a later time. The original was dismantled in 1940 and taken to the campus of the University of Texas, where the permanent fund was fabulously enriched by development that followed the first Santa Rita.

The boomtown lifestyle of which Mrs. Stowe tells is long gone. She realized by the late 1930s, when she was a young woman living and working in Odessa, that this unique experience had already passed into history. For the most part it is unlamented, for it was undeniably hard. But it had compensations which shine forth in this book, chief of them a strong sense of fellowship and generosity among those people who endured it together, a pride in being what some bigoted outsiders disdainfully labeled as "oil field trash."

Whether they realized it or not, theirs was the last act in the drama of this country's frontier experience.

Elmer Kelton
San Angelo, Texas

Preface

I WAS A PIONEER OIL FIELD CHILD. I grew up with the westward progress of the Texas oil industry, moving with my parents from one Texas boomtown to another, with a sojourn in Oklahoma for good measure. I never realized my life differed from that of the ordinary child until I was grown.

Countless other children like me inhabited boomtowns before schools, churches, sometimes even post offices were established. A good number of them were my friends and classmates at one time or another.

We learned early in life to deal with an endless procession of trying circumstances, attempting daily to adjust to changing situations as we accompanied our parents along the crude oil trail.

Pioneer oil field life has been depicted in fact, fiction and movies with emphasis, always, on the lawless fringe element of the population, but I have never read a realistic story of a normal early-day oil field family. That's why I'm telling my story.

Estha Briscoe Stowe
Irving, Texas

This story is as true and as accurate as my memory and research can make it. In a few instances I have supplied a name for a character whose identity neither memory nor research could supply.

EBS

Dedicated to my family,
ANN, JOHN and *DICK*

Here I am at the age of five in a pink and blue dress my mother made for me with long white stockings and high button shoes.

Mexia, Texas
1921

IT WAS RAINING ON "TENT TOWN" just outside the Mexia city limits, where rows of army-style peaked-top tents erected over wooden floors were the only housing available to families of oil field workers.

Each tent was furnished with a kerosene cookstove, a wooden table, a few cane-bottom chairs and assorted beds, cots and mattresses. An outside hydrant served six or eight families. Several unpainted outhouses with doors marked "M" or "W" completed the living arrangements provided by some enterprising landlord who recognized the chance to make a killing for a small investment.

A muddy parking area at the end of the double row of tents held a hodgepodge of Model T Fords, flatbed trucks, and a few stripped-down hoopies. As work shifts changed on the nearby drilling rigs several of the cars departed carrying men in clean overalls with black tin lunchpails. This process went on twenty-four hours a day, seven days a week, with no time off for weekends, holidays or vacations.

The year was 1921, and I was five years old. It had been raining for weeks and our tent, though it did not really leak, emitted a light mist, moistening everything inside it. Our trunks and suitcases, packed with damp clothes, stood open on the wet floor. Last night my father had said, "I quit today. We're getting out of this mudhole."

I stood on a wooden box beside the kerosene stove watching Mother fry eggs and bacon in a black, sheet-iron skillet. She flipped grease on the eggs to "close their eyes." I was bundled into a coat and cap and wore a pair of black rubber boots with red bands just under my knees.

Mother had gathered her long auburn hair under a blousy faille dustcap that matched the touring duster she wore over her clothing, as if she anticipated a long ride down a dusty road. Today she wore it to keep her dry. Her dainty feet and ankles were clamped into a pair of men's galoshes.

My father, a short muscular man in a yellow slicker jacket, was transferring a pan of biscuits from the oven to a bowl on the oilcloth-covered table. His six-foot brother, my Uncle Arthur, sat hunched beneath the table, putting on his shoes and socks.

Uncle Arthur had bunked with other men in a tent near us, taking his meals with us until the night before last when someone stole the suitcase from beneath his cot, leaving him with only the clothes he wore.

"Aren't you a little crowded under there?" my father asked, laughing.

"Yes, but it's the only dry spot in the house," Uncle Arthur replied.

After breakfast the trunks and cases were closed, and I rode on my father's back as he carried a suitcase in each hand. We made our way to the parking lot through mud and water, striving to stay on the mud-covered boxing boards someone had laid down until we reached an open touring car where a man waited with the car's engine running.

The car lurched and spun its wheels as it followed the deep ruts dug out by truck and wagon wheels. Finally we reached a railroad station and boarded a train where it was warm and dry.

"Where are we going?" I asked.

"To Grandmother Briscoe's house," Mother answered.

"When will we come back?" I wanted to know. She cast her brown eyes toward my father, waiting for him to answer.

"Not till it stops raining," he said. All the adults laughed at this, so I laughed too. As yet I was unaware of the oil-field adage, "Every drop of oil that flows from the ground brings a corresponding drop of rain from the sky." The adults had seen this proven in Mexia, and they were escaping the proof.

I'm not sure how long it rained in Mexia, but it was not raining there three years later when my parents and I returned. Uncle Arthur never went back.

This is my first fragmentary memory of the oil fields. I do not remember reaching my grandparents' farm near Pecan Gap, Texas, this particular time but visits there was always joyous occasions. I also loved to visit my mother's family in Brady. My grandfather was a flour miller there and also a neighborhood grocer. I had countless aunts, uncles and cousins in both places.

My mother was christened Effie Alvina Bumgardner but her family shortened it to Vina. My father never called her anything but "Viney." He loved to call her "My tiny Viney" for she was a very petite woman.

Vina suffered a traumatic girlhood, watching her mother slowly die of consumption at the age of thirty-seven. At that time, though she was only sixteen, Vina had to leave school and shoulder the responsibility of her father's house and her younger brother and sister, Sylvester and Lela. An older sister, Lillie, had married earlier, leaving Vina the oldest child still at home. Vina, who had been an excellent student, never quite recovered from the disappointment of leaving school.

At the time of his wife's death, W. T. Bumgardner operated a small coal mine in a rural community called Waldrip, a few miles from Brady. The Briscoe family lived on a nearby farm, and that is how Vina and John met.

He courted her for several years, but she could not desert her father, sister and brother. Finally, in 1913, when Vina and John were both twenty-three, they decided to be married, even though it meant taking Sylvester and Lela to live with them.

3

After a few years Lela went to Fort Worth to finish school and study secretarial work, but Sylvester, called Buss, never wandered far from Vina's side.

Vina and John lived near Waldrip, raising cotton and feed on a sharecropper basis until after my birth in 1916. By this time, my grandfather Bumgardner had moved to Brady and the Briscoe family soon relocated in the blackland farming area of East Texas.

My father, John Briscoe, was fourth in a family of nine children. The Briscoes were a joyful, working, singing tribe. When he married Vina, they gathered her to their hearts and gave her the love and happiness she had missed in her girlhood. John had learned both farming and carpentry from his father and both occupations offered a frugal livelihood at that time. Opportunities in other lines of work were scarce because World War I was over and thousands of former soldiers were looking for work. Any job was considered a good one.

When stories of oil field work, paying five dollars a day for unskilled labor, reached my father's ears he felt compelled to give it a try.

"At that rate," he reasoned, "I can save enough to set myself up in a business of my own." He had once worked for Donnelly and Walker Grocery Company in Henrietta, Texas, and hoped to have such a store of his own.

That's how we became an itinerant oil field family.

Ardmore, Oklahoma
1921 – 1922

OKLAHOMA'S FALL RAINS had set in when we reached Ardmore and moved, temporarily, into a vacated farmhouse on the leases of Amerada Petroleum Company. My father was a connection gang pusher. His crew of six men installed pipe linking Amerada's newly-completed wells to huge oil storage tanks. My mother's brother, who also worked for Amerada, lived with us.

My Uncle Buss was a clerk at the tool shed, responsible for issuing tools, gasoline and other supplies to workers for use in various parts of the field.

I was lonely living at the farmhouse. There were no neighbors, and I saw only the three adults from day to day. My only entertainment was watching the trucks and teams of horses hauling heavy equipment that passed along just beyond the wide front porch. Nothing traveled that road without my scrutiny.

Hearing a noise out front one morning, I hurried to look out the window. I saw two muddy figures in the road slugging away at each other. One man kept knocking the other down, waiting for him to get up, then knocking him down again.

"A fight! A fight!" I shouted, glad for any excitement to break the monotony.

My mother looked out the window. Despite the mud that covered the men, even dripping from their noses, she instantly recognized the form of her brother. She had pulled him from too many fights in his lifetime to be fooled by a little slush.

"Buss! Buss!" She ran out the door shouting, "Buss, stop it!"

Oil flows over a derrick in Oklahoma, 1921.

Then, seeing that I was following her, she called over her shoulder, "Go back in the house and shut the door."

I moved back regretfully, just inside the door but could not bring myself to shut out all those marvelous cusswords the men shouted at each other. Mother didn't really stop the fight. It stopped of its own accord when my uncle knocked the other fellow into a water-filled rut and he couldn't get up.

"Why did you fight that guy?" I asked my swollen-faced uncle at the supper table that night.

"Because that thievin' S.O.B. is stealin' gas from Amerada and makin' my tool shed accounts come up short every damned week."

My mother rolled her eyes heavenward and shook her head. She had never been able to make him leave off profanity in my presence.

"You're going to get fired!" She said it with such vehemence that I assumed she hoped he would.

This errant brother was in his early twenties. He was not a

Aunt Ira, in her high button shoes, admires the new suit Mother has just tailored for herself.

Aunt Ira tied a ribbon around my head and gave me the giggles.

large man but was quite muscular. The handsome dark features that revealed his German ancestry took on a stormy look when he became angry, which was often. He seldom spoke, flew off the handle easily and was quick to engage his fists. This troubled Mother greatly.

At this point she shouldn't have worried. He left us for a while, then returned bringing a bride. They rented a cabin near us, and I never heard of him having another fight.

His bride's name was Ira, much too masculine a name for a pretty, feminine young lady with heavy dark tresses and hazel eyes. She had eloped with my uncle from a girls' normal school in South Texas, a fact that delighted me after Mother explained the meaning of the word "elope."

This young couple, through the next ten years, played an important part in my life as we moved along together from one boomtown to another.

Our next move was very soon. We moved from the farmhouse to an area of tents where Amerada workers lived. There my father erected a cabin-tent especially designed to withstand the cold weather that would soon come sweeping through Oklahoma.

It was another of the peaked-top tents with a tall center pole to hold up the peak. He bought new lumber to build the floor and walls about four feet high. He laid heavy black tarpaper on the floor and covered it with linoleum. Outside, the wooden walls were covered with heavy canvas, drawn tight to keep the cold wind from finding the cracks.

Inside the tent was divided into three sections by cretonne curtains that slid on wires and could be pushed against the center pole when they were not needed. The largest room was the kitchen-living area, furnished with a kerosene range, a sheet-iron heater that used coal, a table surrounded by three cane-bottom chairs, and a trunk to serve as seating.

Beside the range a large wooden box stood on end to be used for a cabinet. It doubled as a packing box when we moved. Across the room stood Mother's sewing machine, the familiar Singer treadle model, always ready to make clothing, curtains or cushions for the hard chairs. My mother, a gifted seamstress and needle-woman, was seldom without needlework in her hands.

The other two areas were our bedrooms. A cot, trunk and a few toys furnished mine while my parents had an iron bedstead, another trunk and a packing-box dresser with a mirror hung above it. We were cozy through that winter, even when it snowed, but some of our neighbors, who had taken less time and effort to erect their tents, did not fare so well.

Setting up a heating stove, passing a stovepipe through the side of a canvas tent, was risky business requiring special supplies and know-how. Without this special attention tents became serious fire hazards. Many people lost their belongings and some even lost their lives because of haphazardly installed heaters. I witnessed one of these fires just as my father was leaving for work one morning.

I sat in the driver's seat of the Model T Ford, ready to advance and retard the gas and spark levers, the way my father had taught me to do, while he engaged the crooked crank handle in the front of the car just below the radiator and spun it round and round. When the engine fired I had learned to advance the spark and "give 'er the gas." My father then vaulted over the left dummy-door to his seat under the steering wheel while I quickly slid to the other side, kissed him goodbye and slid out the right door.

On this particular morning, just as he called "Give 'er the gas," I saw a tent, directly behind my father and some distance away, erupt into flames. I screamed and pushed both levers to the top. The engine stopped abruptly. I kept screaming, "Look!" and pointing until Daddy looked behind him. A woman ran from the fire with her long winter robe in flames. Daddy began shouting, "Lie down and roll!" but the woman only ran faster, so he ran after her.

Neighbors from other tents hurried to help. Finally, my father and another man caught her and wrapped her in a blanket someone had handed them. They took the woman to the hospital where she died that night. The neighbors in camp shook their heads sadly. They had tried, in vain, to get the owner of the tent to correct his heater installation.

Neighbors in these camps became friends quickly, often out of necessity, and the children did the same. My parents were both friendly people, and our home was open to everyone, young or old. The coffeepot was always full and there was usually cake or cookies ready to serve at a moment's notice.

One of Daddy's co-workers, an ex-soldier we called Slim, tasted Mother's cooking and asked if he could take his evening

Amerada Company tanks and derricks in Oklahoma.

An Oklahoma derrick in the snow.

meals with us. Mother agreed, and Slim became a regular member of our family for a while. He dressed in his uniform once to show us how he looked during the "great war."

Slim was at least six feet tall, and the heavy wool uniform in a dark olive-drab color with shiny brass buttons fit neatly around his lean, hard body. His trouser legs became tight at the knees, and a pair of tight leggings encased his legs from knee to ankle. He wore a round hat with a stiff brim, the same type hat that later became the trademark of Smokey the Bear who cautioned us about forest fires. Slim showed us his gun, too, and the kids in camp gathered around to admire this soldier. He made himself more popular by taking us riding in his new 1921 Ford.

I was especially glad to have lots of children to play with in this camp, for I missed Aunt Ira and Uncle Buss who had recently moved to Duncan. Slim left, too, after a few months, and the kids all missed him.

All spring and summer I played with a blue-eyed, golden-haired girl named Lily, who was two years older than I. Most of the children in camp were somewhat younger, except for Pete, whose age we couldn't determine because he was mentally retarded. We played with everyone who was big enough to run, ride a stickhorse or chase a ball. Pete ran along, imitating our actions.

Pete could laugh and shout but never talked. He had a winning smile, though, and the children accepted him and loved him. We tried to protect him from anything that might harm him.

Oil field kids learned, early, to stay away from all company equipment the way city kids learn to stay out of the streets. Each lease was dotted with tanks, racks of pipe, cable tool drilling rigs, old boilers and other paraphernalia used to discover oil, coax it out of the ground, store it and ship it. There were no fences to keep us out of danger, and our tent homes were always located near some of these things.

Especially dangerous were engines left running permanently

to pump the oil into tanks after a well had been drilled. Boilers, used to provide steam for engines, were also very dangerous, though an attendant was usually nearby. Slush pits were not attended and presented a hazard, especially to curious children. Slush pits were man-made ponds dug to catch the mud and slush out of the hole during the drilling operation. These pits were deep and filled with greasy water and slimy drilling mud.

Steamlines, running from boilers to engines, often on top of the ground, could give your bare foot a nasty burn. Kids, accustomed to walking barefoot on the hot earth, welcomed a nice cool oil pipe like an oasis in the desert, but woe to the child who mistook a steam pipe for an oil pipe. Almost all of us did this at least once, but most of us never stepped on a second steam pipe!

We usually played in the open spaces around our tents and sometimes in the dirt road. Teams of mules did the hauling, and we had plenty of time to get out of their way. We liked to watch teams go by; sometimes sixteen teams of mules would be required to pull the heavy loads of machinery. It was fun to hear the drivers, called mule skinners, as they urged the teams on. Their language was quite as colorful as any the oil field had to offer, but our parents forbade us to repeat it. Trucks and tractors, just coming into use, were much faster but not so much fun to watch.

Lily and I played paper dolls much of every day. We used dolls cut from old mail-order catalogues and kept them inside the tents because the wind played havoc with them. Late in the evening we always played outside with the other kids.

My father sometimes played ball with us for a while when he came home. He laughed and joked with us and had special names for all the kids. There was "Lily of the Valley," "Half-Pint" and "Beech Nut," because the boy actually chewed tobacco with his father and brothers. I was called "Poochie" because, as he told it, "Mother and I had planned to get a dog but we got you instead." It never crossed my mind that he might have preferred the dog.

Slim plays "hold-up" with my dad, using a World War I pistol.

Lily and I sit on Slim's new 1921 Ford.

I'm standing on a boiler wearing my overalls and rubber boots.

One summer evening after supper my parents and I were sitting on the low step at the door of our tent enjoying the summer twilight. An oil well that had recently been completed and put "on the pump" stood just across the way, and as the walking beam moved up and down, it seemed to be squeaking. My father remarked that something needed grease, but Mother thought differently.

"It sounds like someone crying," she said.

We heard it again. I started to run over and take a look, and my father called, "Don't go too near that slush pit."

I ran around the embankment of the pit and saw a head poking up out of the slime. "There's someone in there," I called back. They both hurried toward me.

"It's Pete!" my father exclaimed. He ran straight into the muddy water almost to his armpits. But when he grabbed Pete, the frightened boy began fighting, jerked loose and disappeared under the water. My father dived under, pinned Pete's arms to his sides and picked him up, then struggled through the sticky mud until he reached the embankment. By this time neighbors had heard our shouts and several men appeared. They put Pete over a man's knees and rolled him back and forth as the muddy water flowed from his mouth. Mother took off her apron and wiped the grime from his frightened little face.

About this time Pete's parents arrived. His mother was completely hysterical. She began screaming, "My baby, what have you done to him?" One of the women tried to calm her but failed. Finally she slapped the mother so hard she almost staggered backward off the dike. I was horrified. Why would she slap the poor woman when she was so distressed about her child? To my amazement, Pete's mother calmed down immediately. She and her husband took Pete to a doctor who "pumped out his stomach." I wondered about this for days. I imagined a doctor holding the hose from a tire pump down Pete's throat while he pumped away. I thought that must have been just terrible.

Pete's parents later reported that the doctor had recommended a school where Pete could be taught to talk and possibly many other things they had thought him incapable of learning. I grieved for Pete because he had to leave his parents and go away to school.

By the end of that summer my father had gained quite a reputation for lifesaving. He brushed all praise off with a shrug. "I had to do it," he said. "I was the only one there." This was only one little corner of the oil patch. Such dramas were taking place wherever boomers were congregated.

Not long after Pete's near-drowning another crisis arose, and my curiosity about the stomach pump was satisfied.

One evening just as my father came in from work the very young woman next door came over, carrying her baby in one arm and a drinking glass in the other. The baby, about eighteen months old, was crying and drooling.

"Mr. Briscoe," she said, "do you know what this is in this glass? The baby just drank some of it."

"Smells like battery acid," my father said. "Where did he get it?"

The woman pointed to a Model T sitting beside her tent. The running board was covered with tools and car parts where her husband had left them the night before.

My mother disappeared into our tent and came back bringing the bowl of mashed potatoes from our supper table. She offered the baby huge bites with a tablespoon she had picked up. He kept crying but ate the potatoes hungrily.

"Get in the car. Let's get him to a doctor," my father said, "and keep feeding him. Maybe the potatoes will soak up some of the acid." We all jumped into the car and hurried toward town. Just down the road we met the baby's father walking home from work, so he joined us.

At the doctor's office I saw the stomach pump in action since the adults were too preoccupied with saving the baby's life to no-

A well "on the pump." An early-day method of pumping oil from the earth by utilizing the machinery used in the drilling process. On display at the Petroleum Museum, Midland, Texas. Photo by Dick Stowe.

tice a six-year-old watching it all. I found the doctor's method of pumping the stomach fully as gruesome as the one I had dreamed up.

The doctor's method worked, though. In a few hours, the baby was asleep and could be taken home, but not before the doctor said a few very firm words to the young parents about being careful and taking better care of their infant. The couple hung their heads and admitted they had learned a lesson. We went home to a cold supper without mashed potatoes, happy that the baby was alive.

Supper was always on the table when my father got home. It was a time of day I looked forward to because we discussed the affairs of the day as we ate. Mother and I liked to hear stories of things that happened in the oil field each day, especially those concerning new men who came to work in Daddy's gang and were the subject of many practical jokes before they learned their way around an oil rig.

A teaming crew moving a tank on skids. Arthur C. Flores Collection. Courtesy the Petroleum Museum, Midland, Texas.

Roustabouts had their own terms for many tools and operations used on the rig floor, and a new man, called a greenhorn, had to learn in a hurry if he wanted to survive. One young fellow, fresh from the farm, was sent to the toolhouse for a left-handed monkey wrench. Though it was half a mile to the toolshed, his long legs made it there and back in record time. But he brought nothing in his hands.

"That feller down there says what size do you want?"

"Tell him to send me a four-inch," the pusher replied.

The greenhorn made the trip again, a little more slowly this time. When he returned to the rig floor he pushed his hat back and asked, "Do you want it four inches ID or OD?" (inner diameter or outer diameter).

"Tell him ID," one of the roustabouts instructed him. The greenhorn sighed and turned toward the toolhouse a third time. But he happened to glance back just as he left the rig floor. The men were holding their sides to keep from laughing aloud.

"Aw, heck," said the greenhorn in disgust, "somebody's pulling my leg."

A few days later the crew needed to do a cable repair job and couldn't find the long-handled ladle that was used for heating the soft alloy of tin and copper they called babbitt. The pusher turned to the new fellow and said, "Run down to the toolhouse and get me a yellow dog."

Now this was an accepted name for the tool he wanted, but the young fellow refused to go. "I ran all over this place hunting left-handed monkey wrenches, but nobody's gonna get me to go lookin' for no yellow dog."

Such stories kept our supper hour lively. Then Dad liked to sit on the front step for a while before his early bedtime. That Big Ben alarm clock was sure to cause a ruckus at 5:30 the next morning.

In fall and winter it was dark when my father reached home. Mother had just lighted the kerosene lamp in the middle of the table on one such night when Daddy showed her a letter he had picked up at the Amerada office that day.

"How would you like to move to Duncan? Live near your brother? Fifty cents a day more salary."

Mother grabbed for the letter, but missed.

"And besides that," he continued, "Poochie could go to school."

Mother made a successful grab and began reading the letter.

"I can go to school? Can I really?" I was bouncing in my chair. It was true. Legal school age in Texas was seven, and we had no idea it was six in Oklahoma until Aunt Ira wrote that she had learned this from children living near her. I had been counting the months until I was old enough for school, and now I learned I had already missed a month.

"Buss says there's a job waiting for you, with a company

house," my aunt said in closing. I was too excited to eat, and my parents wore broad smiles too. I knew we would be moving.

"We can save that extra fifty cents a day," my father remarked.

"We should do better than that with no coal to buy. They have gas, water and lights all furnished," said Mother.

"But I'll need money for pencils and paper and crayons and all those things," I reminded them, full of importance at being a schoolgirl at last.

"I think we can handle that," Mother said. "Now eat your supper, and you can help me pack tomorrow."

Two days later we said farewell to all our friends and neighbors. What ever happened to lovely, golden-haired Lily, to Pete, to Half-Pint, Beech Nut and all the rest? I never saw any of them again.

A rack holding an assortment of cable tool bits, bailers and fishing tools. Commonly called "a string of tools." On display at the Petroleum Museum, Midland, Texas. Photo by Dick Stowe.

Duncan, Oklahoma
1922–1923

IT WAS A COLD WINTER. I walked to school down a dusty road with a dozen or more children. We girls wore long union suits reaching to our ankles with black stockings pulled up over them to the knees where the stockings were held in place by the elastic leg bands of our black sateen bloomers. Over all this we wore heavy dresses, sweaters, coats, caps, scarves and mittens. The boys were also bundled for winter weather in stocking caps, sweaters and coats above their heavy knickers and black stockings. The knickers were designed to buckle just below the knee but the buckles usually hung loose and clanged on lunch pails and book satchels as they walked.

Miss Lee taught six grades in the one-room school which, this year, was filled to overflowing. Double desks built for two students had to hold three and, invariably, the one in the center was the one who needed to get a drink or to visit the outhouse on the far corner of the schoolyard.

Despite this obvious overload Miss Lee found time to give me extra help because I had entered late. She soon had me reading right along with the other first graders. I loved to read everything in sight—road signs, oatmeal boxes, coffee cans and baking powder tins.

I dogged the footsteps of Mother and Aunt Ira, spelling out words and asking, "What does that spell?" One afternoon I ran over to my aunt's house just as she returned from the grocery store. As she removed each item from the bag I read its label. At the bottom of the bag I found an unfamiliar box and asked, "What does k-o-t-e-x spell?"

"Where did you see that?" she asked.

"On that blue box."

"Oh, yes," she answered. "Let's put the things away first and I'll tell you about that."

That was the beginning of many lessons she would teach me, lessons my shy mother had asked her to handle.

Aunt Ira and Uncle Buss lived in the first house in the row of six houses; ours was number four. I wore a path across the intervening backyards, for I felt it my duty to stay involved in the happenings of both houses.

The houses, painted gray and white, each had two rooms, with a front and back porch. A small gas range was furnished, along with built-in cabinets and a kitchen sink with a cold-water faucet. There were times when the water pressure was too low to reach the house, and we had to get water at the backyard faucet, but not often. All toilets were outdoors, and baths had to be taken in a number three washtub.

But it was a friendly neighborhood. My parents were happy living there, and I enjoyed every day at school. It was a good time for us all. Too good to last.

Trouble arrived late one afternoon when a man from the company office knocked at our door with a message. "A string of tools fell at old No. 3—Bumgardner is hurt—bad. You'd better get his wife and go to the hospital in Duncan."

Uncle Buss was a gang pusher, and the roustabouts that composed his work crew were his gang. The tons of tools used to service oil wells hung by heavy cables high in the derrick. The cables came from a set of huge bull wheels at the back of the derrick floor, and the tools were lifted into place by power from a steam engine located in the engine room at the far end of the belt house.

On this day a loud crack, high in the derrick, had alerted the men to danger. Someone yelled, "Run!" All the roustabouts made it to the edge of the rig floor and jumped to the ground. The heavy tools crashed through the wooden floor and buried themselves in the ground below. The pusher was carried through the floor with them.

When the frantic men dug him out of the rubble, he appeared to be dead but they rushed him to the hospital anyway. There they found a faint heartbeat.

After several critical days with no improvement, Amerada had a specialist flown in from Tulsa to determine the extent of his injuries. A doctor flown in by airplane! What an event! An oil company that accepted such responsibility was also quite unusual.

The specialist determined that my uncle had one lung crushed, along with all the ribs that covered it. His shoulder and both arms were also broken, but the prognosis was good. He would live. This verdict brought us guarded happiness, for we knew he had a long way to go before he was fully recovered.

Nobody seemed happier to hear the good news than that gang of roustabouts who, despite their wild and reckless image, arrived one at a time to sit by his bedside each night until he was out of danger.

It was several months later when Uncle Buss was able to return to work. According to one of his gang he was met with catcalls.

"Ole Slowpoke is back!"

"Yeah, Ole Molasses in January!"

"We're gonna tie a can to your tail and teach you to run!"

That's when the pusher, reportedly, favored the crew with a lopsided grin and replied, "You S.O.B.s go to Hell!" Things were back to normal in the oil patch.

About this time, at the company camp, our small houses were being readied for company. My Aunt Lela and Uncle Sam Baker from Fort Worth were coming for a visit bringing their two children, Vivian, a little past three, and her baby brother, Billy.

Aunt Lela, my mother's youngest sister was almost a carbon copy of my mother except for her much more peppery personality. She had left her secretarial studies to marry a tall, sandy-haired stonemason whose skilled hands could build a brick wall the way an artist paints a landscape. The Bakers were an attractive couple and so were their children. Vivian had her mother's dark hair and eyes, and the chubby baby, Billy, was dark-eyed too, though his head showed no promise of ever producing hair. I could hardly lift the hefty baby, but I lugged him along everywhere I went, even though he howled lustily all the while. I begged my parents for a little brother just like him, and they agreed, "That would be nice."

Soon after my relatives' visit, I discovered that I had lost a gold ring I had been wearing. It was a Bumgardner family heirloom, having been worn by several children in the family. When I outgrew it, it was scheduled to go to Vivian and on through the family. We all searched for the ring with no success. I simply could not remember where I had it last.

That night Aunt Ira dreamed that she rose and tried to fill her teakettle at the sink, but the water refused to run. She then went out the back door to the hydrant with the teakettle in her hand. There, on a small splashboard beneath the hydrant, lay the ring, half covered with mud.

Next morning she did not remember the dream until the faucet at the sink refused to run. In a flash the dream came back to her. She threw the kettle in the sink and bounded down the back steps. Sure enough, there lay the ring where I had washed my hands after Vivian and I had made mud pies.

It was barely daylight when Aunt Ira came sprinting across the neighbors' backyards, alarming everyone with her cries, "I found it, I found it!"

Soon after this I was given a gold initial ring for my seventh birthday, so I passed the family ring to my cousin. It was a wonderful birthday, for Mother and Aunt Ira gave me the first birthday party I ever had.

We invited two boys and three girls to come home with me after school. We played tag outdoors until Aunt Ira called us in to blindfold us and let us pin the tail on a donkey she had drawn and hung on the door. We thought it hilarious when a little girl pinned the tail on the donkey's ear. Then I was given my ring, and the children gave me presents, too. There were hair ribbons, handkerchiefs, and even a bottle of lilac perfume from the dimestore. After I blew out the candles on my tall white cake, my mother served it along with ice cream from a hand-cranked freezer.

As we ate we discussed the parts Miss Lee had given us that day. We were to learn them for the school closing program, just a little over a month away. We knew we had to work hard to learn them.

The weather was warm most of the time now, but our mothers refused to let us leave off that heavy underwear. It was cool in the mornings, but by afternoon we had removed our shoes and long black stockings, rolling the legs of the union suits up under the sateen bloomers. We squished the loose dust of the lane between our toes all the way home. It felt heavenly!

At last all our practicing was over and the night of the school closing program had arrived. Parents and students overflowed the one-room school as we sang patriotic songs, spoke our pieces, and bowed while our parents applauded.

My speech was "If" by Rudyard Kipling. Though I understood little of its message, I had worked for weeks to commit the lengthy poem to memory and to speak each word just as Miss Lee directed. As I recited the rhythmical work, I felt the attention of the audience. By the time I received their applause, I was hooked for life. I became an incurable ham that night.

After the program I said goodbye to each schoolmate and my teacher, promising to see them in the fall when I would be in the second grade. But I broke the promises I made that night. Before the summer was over, the Pure Oil Company had need of two gang pushers in the Mexia, Texas, field. We were native Texans, and the adults wanted to go back to Texas.

I never saw those wonderful friends again.

Mexia Again
1923–1925

IT WAS AUGUST WEATHER IN MEXIA. The tent city looked the same except the mud was gone. The sun beat down on the ragged peaked-top tents and heavy dust rose each time a car passed along the dirt road we had used three years before. Thankfully, we did not live in tent city this time. We had found a two-room cabin-and-tent combination for rent on the Pure Oil lease.

The cabin sat in a grove of trees at the end of a lane where grapevines climbed every tree trunk and completely enveloped a fence, posts and all.

The Bumgardners needed a cabin, too. They came from Oklahoma with us, hauling our furniture and theirs on a small flat-bed truck. Our car was loaded with boxes and small household items tied to the running boards. The back seat was stacked high with suitcases, so I rode in the front seat between my parents, who constantly reminded me to "sit down and be still."

The five of us crowded into our two-room cabin while the search went on for a cabin for my aunt and uncle. A row of make-shift cabins and tents lined the lane leading to Mr. Boggs's grocery store but they were all occupied. Half a mile from the store stood a wooden lean-to that sheltered children as they waited for the Forest Glade school bus. I was anxious to meet the children who lived along the lane and to ride that yellow bus.

A day or two after our arrival Uncle Buss assisted the search for a house by bringing home a real good second-hand Ford for Aunt Ira to drive.

"Vina," he said, "you've taught this girl to make buttermilk biscuits and cobbler pies. Now I want you to teach her to drive her car."

"Sure," said my mother. "We can drive and look for a house at the same time."

"But don't take Estha with you." He winked at me. "I don't want her all crippled up." He knew that nothing could have kept me out of that car.

Teaching my aunt to drive proved easier than finding a suitable cabin to rent, but the two women, in time, accomplished both tasks. The cabin was two or three miles from ours and could only be reached by a narrow road over a steep hill. The road was so rough that it rattled our teeth together when the little Ford struggled to the top and rumbled down the other side.

As soon as the men left for work one morning I was asked to help the women load the car with some of the smaller boxes as well as mops, brooms, buckets and a big bottle of Lysol disinfectant. We were going to clean the cottage before the men came along after work, bringing the truck with the furniture.

Mother rode up front, holding a kerosene lamp to keep it safe. I occupied a small nook in the back seat beside a box of pots and pans. Aunt Ira was confidently manning the steering wheel. We chugged up the hill with pots, pans, buckets and mop handles banging against each other. I was admonished to "keep those pans quiet," but there was no way I could stop the clatter.

At last we reached the top of the hill and started down the other side. Aunt Ira, confused by the clatter and the rocky road that bounced us like jumping beans, felt that she was driving too fast. Unconsciously she pulled up on the steering wheel as she would have pulled on the reins to stop a horse. This did not slow the car, but the steering wheel slipped off the steering column and left her twisting it madly in the air with no control of the car.

Seeing her predicament Mother cried, "Stop, stop!" Aunt Ira

stamped down quickly with both feet, and the car stopped with one great crash of pots and pans.

The car had not left the road, no harm had been done, but Aunt Ira still sat, ghost-white, twisting the useless wheel in her hands as if she had frozen there.

My mother looked the situation over calmly and then began to laugh. She laughed until tears ran down her face. Gradually Aunt Ira relaxed a little. She let the useless wheel down, smiled a wan smile, and asked, "What shall I do with my real good second-hand Ford now, Vina?"

We found that she could replace the wheel on the steering column and insert the square metal pin that had fallen into her lap. Using a small rock from the plentiful supply in the road, Aunt Ira tapped the metal pin into place, and we rattled on down the road.

With the Bumgardners settled and our own house in order, I went out to make friends with the gang of kids along the lane. We numbered more than a dozen, and we spent the rest of the summer playing under the leafy trees and swinging in grapevine swings. When fall came and the grapes hung juicy and ripe, we learned to let them hang because, despite their sweet taste, they left our lips, tongues and throats burning painfully. Some of the mothers tried making pies and jellies with the beautiful fruit. Even these things had a definite bite.

Each child had to have a try at smoking pieces of grapevine only to find it made clear blisters on the lips and tongue. We settled for swinging.

Outdoor toys were scarce with this group. There were no bicycles or tricycles. A few children had balls, and old shovel handles made good bats. Most of the time we improvised with whatever became available. We used empty tomato or corn cans along with pieces of baling wire to make tin-can walkers. With a foot on each can and each hand holding a wire loop, we could "walk tall" and cut little round circles in the hard dirt.

The more daring youngsters built stilts out of one-by-four boards, nailing wooden blocks on to make a stirrup. Some of the bigger boys became quite sure-footed on these, and they competed to see who could build the tallest.

These same big boys found a length of cable one day and built a trolley between two trees. To ride the trolley one climbed the tree where the cable was tied highest, held to a piece of overall ducking wrapped around the cable to protect the hands, and slid down the cable to the lower end which was tied to a second tree not far away.

This trolley was especially high, even on the lower end, so it was necessary to judge your distance and drop to the ground before reaching the second tree. Big boys managed this fine but kept bragging that it was far too dangerous for the girls or smaller boys. Most of us accepted this but not Zelma.

Zelma, a girl of about twelve and a confirmed tomboy, was not about to miss out on this fun, so she caught the boys unaware and climbed the tree. All the children began yelling, "No!" and "Don't do it!" But she grabbed the handhold, swung her weight to the cable and was propelled downward at top speed. She failed to turn loose at the critical time and slammed, full length, into the tree. Then she fell to the ground limp as a rag doll, knocked out cold. The big boys quickly melted away into the woods.

Zelma's mother revived her with a cold wet cloth to her face, but an angry knot appeared on her forehead, and she had skins and bruises all over her arms and legs. That night Zelma's father tore down the trolley and threatened, "I'll skin the skunk that puts it back up."

Zelma had lived there the year before and was the oldest of the girls along the lane. She shepherded us all to school on the first day, the same as she did her smaller siblings. Most of us had moved here recently from some other oil field. Zelma felt important that day. "Bossy" is what the kids called her, along with

I visited the Forest Glade School near Mexia in 1967 and recalled my happy second- and third-grade days.

"smart aleck" and several other uncomplimentary names, but we younger children felt a little safer in her care.

Forest Glade was a new two-story red brick school located in a lovely green glade several miles from Mexia. It was the largest building I had ever seen, and it was the first time I had ever seen a schoolroom with only one grade. The teacher lacked Miss Lee's youth and charm, but I soon adjusted to all the changes.

A few days into the school term Mother asked one evening, "Guess who I saw in the grocery store today?"

"Dunno—who?" asked Daddy.

"Della McCrorey."

"You don't say! Do they live here?"

I broke in to ask, "Who's Della McCrorey?"

"She's Daddy's cousin, and they live at the dairy just beyond the school bus stop."

"Tom McCrorey running a dairy?" My father shook his head

in disbelief. He and Mother agreed that we should visit the long-lost cousins right after supper.

"Do they have any children?" I wanted to know.

My mother smiled broadly as she answered, "Four girls, and they are your second cousins."

"Oh boy!" I shouted. I didn't care if they were fourteenth cousins. I would have four more girls for playmates.

Billie McCrorey was about my age, Lynn J. and Florene were a little older, and Martha Jane was about five months old. Lynn's dark hair and creamy white skin gave her a china-doll look. Both she and short, dark-haired Billie wore Buster Brown haircuts with bangs. Flo was a tall, angular girl with darkish blonde hair, long legs, and knees that were always skinned. Martha Jane showed promise of being a brunette, for her eyes were dark and so was the baby fuzz we kept trying to tie with hair ribbons.

We struck up friendships in a hurry. After all, we were relatives and in my family this made a lot of difference. The girls and I decided to call each others' parents "Aunt" and "Uncle" rather than the cumbersome "Cousin This-or-That." That night marked the first of many happy times we would spend together.

We rode the school bus every day and played together almost every afternoon. We often joined the kids along the lane but had our best times when there were just cousins present.

The McCrorey girls loved play-acting as much as I did. Lynn always played the mother, tomboy Flo was the daddy who went to work "pulling oil wells" or climbing to the top of an imaginary derrick. Billie and I were the two mean little kids, constantly being chased by Mother Lynn with a broomweed switch.

The rooms of our playhouse were outlined on the ground with rocks and sticks. We always had a bedroom and bath for each family member, plus a kitchen, dining room, music room, living room, drawing room, library, and an office for the daddy. Our imaginary furniture was as elaborate as our four minds could con-

Dellon, my little "brother-cousin,"
born in Mexia, Texas.

jure up from our limited visits to fine homes or furniture stores.
Being oil field kids and living in tents did not inhibit our dreams.

If Martha Jane happened to be awake, she was our little prin
cess, and we built her a fairy tale nursery. Once we made her an
elaborate bed from old blankets in a hollow tree. Then we couldn't
get her out without hurting her, so Aunt Della had to rescue her.

I had a busy fall going to school, playing with all these friends
and cousins, and visiting the Bumgardners. Christmas was fun
that year, but it was just after Christmas that I got the best surprise
of all. Aunt Ira went to the hospital in Mexia and brought home a
baby boy named Dellon Edward Bumgardner.

They brought him straight from the hospital to our house.
Aunt Ira placed him on my bed and unfolded his blue blanket to
show him to me. He was so tiny! One hand with five perfect little
fingers waved before his face while the other formed a pink ball of

a fist and went into his mouth. Two miniature feet in blue booties kicked the blanket away, and he blinked at the strong light. He had a tiny bit of peach fuzz for hair, and Mennen's baby powder had him smelling as sweet as he looked.

"Well, here is that little brother you've always wanted," she said.

"Mother said he's my little cousin," I stammered.

"Yes," she agreed, "but we're going to let him grow up just like your little brother." From that time I felt that he truly belonged to me.

Aunt Ira was true to her word. She taught me to hold him, rock him and to feed him orange juice with a spoon. I forgot about dolls and played with him every minute he was awake. I spent every possible moment at the little house over the hill, even spending the night there often.

Inevitably the day came when I asked where this wondrous creature came from. Aunt Ira then brought out a large book bound in red leather. She called it her doctor book, because it contained full-page illustrations of the human body and all its organs. She read the text to me, rewording it in terms I could understand.

That's also when she explained to me that I should not keep asking my parents for a brother or sister because it was impossible for Mother to have more children, a fact that made them both sad. I never asked again. With my new little cousin I didn't need one now.

I also promised not to discuss the lessons I had learned from the doctor book with any of my playmates—ever. And I never did.

January and February kept all us oil field kids in raincoats and rubber boots, for the rain had returned to Mexia. By the time March went out "like a lamb" we were removing stockings and shoes and rolling up those union suits again, glad that barefoot weather was not far away.

Busy as I was this term I managed to have my first romance. My beau's name was Joe, and he had red hair and freckles. He was a typical all-American second grader.

Joe often sat beside me on the school bus, declaring to all who would listen that I was his girl. One day he stopped at Mr. Boggs's store on the way home from school and bought me a bag of penny candies. We trudged along the lane sharing the candy with each other but not with the other kids, while the kids teased and taunted us. Finally one of them yelled, "Joe gave you candy. Why don't you kiss him?"

"Shut up," we both answered.

"I dare you," one yelled.

"I double dare you," another called out. With that I turned and gave Joe a resounding smack. His face flamed as red as his hair, and a shout went up from all the kids, except Zelma. She threw her hands over her mouth, and her face registered shock.

"Oh, oh. I'm gonna tell on you," she shouted as she shot past her own house and ran straight to mine. She burst into the room where Mother and Aunt Ira were sewing and made her announcement. As I entered the door she swept past me declaring, "You're gonna get into trouble." She then continued, regally, back to her own house.

"What did she say?" I asked the two surprised women. Aunt Ira was suddenly very busy cutting a thread and rethreading her needle, biting her bottom lip all the while. Finally Mother found words.

"She said you kissed Joe."

"I did."

"Why?"

"Because he gave me candy." This was surely an adequate reason.

"That was kind of him, but nice girls don't kiss boys," she replied.

35

"But I always kiss Charlie and Homer and Jack and Wayne and Edwin Junior . . . "

"They're your cousins and uncles," she reasoned.

"Is cousins all I can kiss?" I wanted to know.

"Well," she stammered, "just don't kiss anybody on the way home from school."

"Why not?"

"Well, you'll get germs," she finished a little lamely.

"Who's got germs?" I asked.

"All of you kids," she shot back. "You're all so dirty by the time you get off that bus that you're bound to have germs." I looked into the mirror hanging above the packing-box dresser, searching for evidence of germs, but she gave me no time to deny their existence.

"Go wash your face and hands. I hear Dellon waking up." That ended the subject.

The romance soon ended anyway. Joe loaned me a marble to bounce on the school sidewalk like the other girls were doing at recess, and I bounced it too hard. It broke in two pieces. I was afraid Joe would be angry, so I told him I lost it in the grass. When I refused to help him hunt for it and told him I would get my daddy to give me a nickel to buy him another marble, he went stomping off. The romance was over.

I had no time to grieve. It was moving time again. This time we moved into a vacant company bunkhouse. It was on the same Pure Oil Company lease but now I caught the school bus at another place. I continued playing with Zelma and the other kids at school every day, but I missed riding the bus with them.

The bunkhouse, with the addition of Mother's curtains and pillows, made us a spacious home. There was a large teaming camp not far from us, a cable tool drilling rig running on a hole just down the road, and another bunkhouse just beside us that had been divided into apartments for two families. Mother planted a handful of castor bean seeds, and the plants were soon growing tall, like shrubs, all around the house. It was a pleasant place to live.

I didn't have to give up my McCrorey cousins, for Uncle Tom and Aunt Della often came over in the evenings to sit on the long side porch with Mother and Dad, while Lynn, Flo, Billie and I acted out fairy tales for their entertainment.

Aunt Della was a slender, fine-featured woman, the daughter of the only minister in our family, my father's Uncle Billy Briscoe. She spoke in a precise and lilting manner and was always cheerful.

Aunt Della sewed for her girls just as my mother did, so they got together and made each of us a long white gown with lace on the shoulders for our fairy-tale games. By adding the lengths of mosquito netting from our beds and a good bit of imagination, we became fairies. We ad-libbed the lines of our favorite stories and took turns playing the different characters. Choice characters, of course, were Cinderella, Rumpelstiltskin, Red Riding Hood and Snow White.

One starry evening a school friend named Nora came to play with us. We gave her the prize role, Cinderella. All went well until Fairy Godmother Flo, with her yardstick-wand, came gliding in, tapped Cinderella on the forehead and asked, "Cinderella, do you want to go to the ball?"

"No," Cinderella replied, "and stop hitting me with that stick!"

Uncle Tom laughed and shouted, "That's the best line in the show."

Uncle Tom was a large, deep-voiced man who prided himself on his part-Indian heritage. I was a little fearful of him, yet I admired him greatly. He built a crystal radio set and treated us to our first sounds from radio. He slipped earphones on each of us, in turn, and we thrilled to the squeaky, crackling tones of classical music coming from some faraway, heretofore unheard-of place.

Next day when I recounted this experience in my classroom, several other children claimed that they too had heard radio music. My teacher, Mrs. Thomas, explained that before very long every family would own a radio and be able to hear musical programs and speeches from all over the world.

I felt sure my family would never own one of these magic boxes. They would belong only to rich people, and my father had said many times, "I don't want to be a rich man. I just want enough money to pay my honest debts and give my child a better education than I got."

My father was sure I was getting that better education, for Forest Glade was a very good school. There was, however, a problem. Children were contracting childhood diseases at an alarming rate. Sometimes a child had two diseases at once or three different diseases, one following the other. Health authorities determined that the school water well was contaminated. For the remainder of the term we brought our own drinking water to school in whatever containers we had available. In most cases, this proved to be quart milk bottles.

School buses full of children armed with book satchels, lunch pails and milk bottles full of water must have given the bus drivers anxiety attacks. Perhaps one out of three bottles reached school intact. Children were cut with the broken bottles, clothing was soaked and the buses ran late because the bus drivers had to stop and handle these emergencies. Once a bottle arrived at school, it had a fifty percent chance of making it through the day.

At first the children kept their bottles on their desks. This was disaster, so bottles were name-tagged and placed on the window ledge where the sun shone through them and we could watch the paper caps slowly disintegrating and floating to the bottom of the bottle in fuzzy little globs.

Children whose bottles got broken had to borrow a drink from the luckier ones who did not dare refuse for they might be in the same predicament tomorrow.

The teachers must have prayed for the term to end. I looked forward to the end of the term also, but for a different reason. The second grade was going to present a play for the school closing program, and Mrs. Thomas had chosen me to play the Queen of Maytime.

In the play the Queen of Maytime presented all the blessings of the springtime, such as flowers, birds, sunbeams, breezes and spring showers. All these spring features were to come dancing onstage in their crepe paper costumes. The queen would wear a long white dress with a train and a silver crown on her head and she would carry a silver scepter.

The days were exciting as we practiced the songs, dances and recitations that were part of the play. With typical seven-year-old egotism I assumed that my ability to memorize and recite poetry had secured the part for me. Whatever ability I had might have been given some consideration, but I'm sure having a mother who was willing to spend days at the sewing machine making a white organdy dress with a million gathered ruffles certainly did not hurt my chances.

All the students were asked to save the foil wrappers from their chewing gum to cover the crown and scepter. (Many years would pass before rolls of aluminum foil were found in every kitchen.) I urged all my friends to chew lots of gum, for I wanted that crown to sparkle.

Alas, I lost my own sparkle just three weeks before the program. I finally succumbed to the epidemic of diseases by taking measles and diphtheria at the same time. I was devastated. I would miss my big chance in show business.

After my diphtheria crisis passed I began to improve. By the middle of the second week I was hopeful that I could attend the last week of school. That's when I took the mumps.

Mumps did not make me very sick. Both jaws were swollen and I had to avoid tart foods, but I felt fine and wanted to go to school. The other children were gradually returning, and they had

39

started practicing the play again. Mrs. Thomas wrote a note to Mother:

"If she feels good enough, send her on to school. She can't possibly expose anyone to anything."

So I went to school on Friday and that evening I wore that white organdy dress. My gum wrapper-covered crown and wand sparkled magically, and I recited my lines with cheeks bulging fat and rosy. I reigned for one glorious evening as Forest Glade's May-time Queen with Mumps.

Mother took me to the doctor for the last time the next week. He pronounced me well but thought my mother looked tired out. He gave her a tonic and suggested that she rest an hour or two each day. After what she'd been through that last month of school, nobody was surprised that she was tired.

The tonic helped Mother some, but she continued to lose weight and feel exhuasted. Daddy thought she needed cheering up, so he suggested a night on the town. After he got off work on Saturday night, we would go to a restaurant for dinner and then to a show at the Opera House.

"Oh, good," I cried. "Will there be real people?"

"Yes," he answered. "First a stage play, then some vaudeville acts, then a moving picture show."

I thought Saturday would never come.

Dinner at a restaurant was a treat for us. Mother and I always ordered tenderloin of trout with tartar sauce. I always asked for a glass of milk just to hear the waitress say, "I'm sorry, but this restaurant does not serve milk and fish together."

For some reason many people believed that a combination of milk and fish became poison. My father declared that he'd caught fish all his life, and Grandmother had always served it with milk, and nobody ever got sick. Nevertheless, we had to abide by the rules.

We reached the Opera House in time to see a comedy-drama

by a traveling dramatic troupe. This was my favorite. Then the dazzling chorus line of dancing girls in feather costumes and hip-length black mesh stockings heralded the start of the vaudeville acts. There were singers, tap dancers, stand-up comedians and jugglers. There was a magician who borrowed a watch from a man in the audience, beat it to pieces with a hammer, then somehow found it again in a locked box, all safe and unscarred.

Mary Pickford was the star of the moving picture, a sad story about orphans. It made me cry, and they moved the dialogue under the picture too fast for me to read it. Mother tried to read it for me but someone behind us said, "Shhh!" so I laid my head in her lap and went to sleep.

Mother said she enjoyed the evening of entertainment, but we could all see that it had no lasting effect on her health. The doctor gave her several different tonics through the summer to keep her going, and she kept pushing herself to keep her housework done. The housecleaning was hard these days.

The cable tool well being drilled down the road from us was about to reach the depth where pay dirt was expected. Cars, wagons and trucks passed along the dirt road in a steady stream, making it necessary for us to close the windows on the east and south to keep out the dust. Mother mopped and dusted constantly.

My dad and I often took a walk down to the rig after supper. Dad liked to talk and joke with the men, and we both became well-acquainted with Mr. McDonald, a man in his forties who fired the boiler to furnish steam for the engine. Work went on around the clock now, each man working a twelve-hour shift. Mr. McDonald worked from noon until midnight. He was usually eating his supper from a black lunch pail while he talked to us in the late evenings, but even as he ate he kept a close eye on the pressure gauge because with a full head of steam that gauge must remain steady.

My parents and I had learned to sleep with the noise from the drilling rig, but one morning around 3:00 A.M. a tremendous explosion shook the house, rattled dishes in the cupboard and sent two window panes crashing to the floor. I sat up in bed just as my father's feet hit the floor and he exclaimed, "My God, the boiler blew!" He jumped into his trousers and shot out the door.

Mother and I huddled, shivering from fright, on the porch. We heard shouts and cries from men, but all drilling noise had stopped. Cars rushed past, headed for town; an ambulance hurried toward the scene with a red light flashing. We wondered why it did not return.

Cars had begun leaving the scene when my father came trudging out of the darkness and dropped wearily on the porch beside us. His body was shaking as in a chill when Mother put her arms around him. His sobs shook his entire body. I was terrified, but Mother asked gently, "How many were killed?"

"Just McDonald," he sobbed. "They picked . . . they picked him up . . . in . . . pieces."

"But McDonald should have gone off duty at midnight," Mother said.

"Yes, I know. His relief didn't show up. He'd been there fifteen hours . . . probably fell asleep."

The light of morning was beginning to show when Mother said, "Let's go in and make some coffee. You'll feel better after you have some breakfast."

"Nothing's going to make me feel better," Daddy declared. "This is one hell of a way to make a living, and if I didn't have to do it, I'd never work another day in a damned oil field." He followed her inside, ate his breakfast and went to work.

I felt sick at heart worrying about him all day, but when suppertime came he was a little quiet but otherwise normal. By morning he was whistling and singing as usual.

The summer moved along with Mother making regular visits to the doctor. She took me with her in late August for a pre-school

I'm standing in front of a boiler with my dad (hands on hips) and a fellow worker.

check-up. The doctor called me "sound as a dollar" and ready for school to begin. Mother insisted the he see a new trick I had learned, so he followed us out to the sidewalk where I showed him the most excellent cartwheel I could manage.

"Doctor, will she shake up her brains or something doing that?" Mother asked.

The doctor laughed and said, "Oh, no. It'll keep her blood circulating. It's good for her."

"But it isn't ladylike," Mother objected.

"Let her be a tomboy while she can," he said. "She'll have to act like a lady soon enough." Then he gave Mother a bottle of cough syrup for the cough she had developed, and we went home.

Aunt Ira was concerned about leaving the area with Mother feeling no better, but Uncle Buss was transferred to a lease near Corsicana. He built a small cabin from brand new boxing boards and the first Sunday it was completed, we had a holiday of sorts. Aunt Lela and Uncle Sam came to see us, and we all gathered at the Bumgardners' new little house.

A dark-haired, brown-eyed girl named Louise had come to join Vivian and Bill in the Baker family by this time, so Vivian and I had two babies to play with while the adults caught up on family gossip. Six adults and five children ate Sunday dinner in that one-room house. It didn't seem crowded to me, but, as hostess, Aunt Ira probably held a different opinion.

After the Bakers had gone, Aunt Ira called me aside and said, "Honey, help your mother all you can. She doesn't seem any better to me."

"She isn't," I replied. "Will you look in the doctor book and read about coughs?"

"I've already read everything I can find about them, but so many things cause them."

"What causes most of them?"

"Colds and bronchitis seem to be the most common, but we just have to follow the doctor's orders."

All the way home I wondered about this. Mother did not have a cold so, I reasoned, it must be the other—bronchitis.

It was time for school to start, but I was torn. I did not want to leave Mother alone during the long day but I was, as always, excited about going to school, especially going back to Forest Glade.

My third-grade teacher, Miss Agnes Unger, was a beautiful, dark-haired young woman who evidently loved children. She praised our good work, causing us to work harder just to please her. She was forever bringing us little surprises that she had ordered from coupons she found in magazines. When we saw her coming from the teacherage with that familiar green wastebasket in her hands, we knew it was full of goodies for us.

Sometimes it was a miniature tube of toothpaste for each child, and along with it came a lesson on dental care. Another day she brought tiny boxes of shoe polish and taught us how to polish our school shoes. There were combs, bars of soap, bottles of shampoo and once she brought tiny cans of Old Dutch Cleanser for us to give our mothers.

When other teachers gathered on the playground to talk while they watched the children play, Miss Unger could be found playing jacks with the girls or spinning tops with the boys.

One sunny day Mr. Joe Thomas, our principal, sent her word that an airplane was visible from the north schoolyard. Miss Unger called out, "Run, see the airplane" and proceeded to lead the way, running as fast as the children.

It was the first airplane I had ever seen, and it flew quite low. We all waved and screamed as if the pilot could hear us. The plane gave a little side-to-side wobble, and Mr. Thomas exclaimed, "Look, he's waving at us "

When the plane was out of sight, Mr. Thomas had us all go into the auditorium for a lesson on airplanes. He told us how they had been used in the World War and were now being used for many things such as transporting important mail. I remembered that a doctor had been flown in one to attend my uncle when he was hurt. Now I knew what one really looked like.

Mr. Thomas finished by saying, "Someday soon we will all travel by air from city to city, even from country to country across

45

mountains and oceans." It all seemed like a fairy tale to me, but it was an exciting day at school. Such good teachers kept school interesting for me all that fall and winter.

Around midnight one November night Mother woke us with a bad spell of coughing. Daddy lit the lamp, and I ran to get a wet cloth to put on her face. She held the cloth to her mouth, and when she took it away it was red with blood. We slept very little the rest of the night and reached the doctor's office before it opened the next morning.

I sat in the doctor's waiting room for hours, it seemed. Daddy came out once to tell me, "They're taking x-rays. Maybe it won't be much longer." The room had filled with people waiting to see the doctor when my parents finally came out. I could see that Mother had been crying and Daddy's face was gray and grim. An ice-cold rock formed in my stomach.

"What is it?" I cried.

"Doctor Porter will talk to you about it," said my father. Then I saw that the doctor was following them. He sat in the chair beside me and took one of my hands in his.

"Honey," he began, "your mother has tuberculosis. We are going to send her to a special hospital where the doctors and nurses know just how to make her well."

"Where is the hospital? Is she going right now—today?"

"No, it may be a few weeks or maybe months before they have an opening. The hospital is near San Angelo."

I'd never heard of San Angelo before. "Why can't she go to a hospital here?"

"Because tuberculosis patients need a high, dry climate," he answered.

"Will we move there?" I asked, more to my father than to the doctor.

"We don't know that yet," my father answered. "We have to keep her in bed and take care of her until they're ready for her. Do you think we can do that?" His gray-blue eyes challenged me.

"Sure we can," I declared. Then I took Mother's hand to show that I was ready to begin.

Daddy and I learned to cook the foods Mother needed, to sterilize dishes, hands and clothing. We kept a record of her temperature and gave her medication day and night. I could not know, of course, the utter despair my parents must have felt, knowing that tuberculosis was the same as "consumption," the malady that had robbed my mother of her girlhood while it slowly took her mother's life. Now it was threatening her own life. Neither of them ever revealed such thoughts to me. Both acted as if she would be well in a short while, and life went on as usual.

Mother felt better at times, since she was not using her energy to keep house. She would not hear of my staying out of school, and our living demanded that Daddy work, so she stayed alone all day. A kind neighbor came in to fix her lunch. I discussed these problems with Miss Unger, and she helped me do my homework assignments at school so that I could give Mother all my attention after school.

"Just practice being an optimist," was Miss Unger's advice.

"What's an optimist?" I asked.

"It's a person who keeps cheerful and believes that everything will work out fine."

"But—will things work out fine?"

"Yes, they will." She was positive. "We all have troubles, but they never last—always try to remember that."

Afterwards each time I remembered her words I felt better, but it was hard to remember them, especially on the nights when Daddy sent me to bed at my regular time and I lay awake, listening

47

as he washed our clothes on a rub-board and hung them out in the cold, dark night. At these times the icy rock in my stomach grew too large for me to sleep until he was in bed also.

I felt better about everything when my Aunt Verna and Uncle Burney Wright came to live with us. Whether my father asked them to come or they chose to come of their own accord, I do not know, but the arrangement was mutually beneficial.

Aunt Verna was my father's sister. The Wrights had lived on a ranch in New Mexico until Uncle Burney was thrown from a horse and a cactus thorn became imbedded under his kneecap. Surgery left his knee stiff and bent at about a forty-five degree angle, causing him to limp badly. Since he could no longer manage a ranch, they decided to try to get college educations so that both could become teachers.

Uncle Burney could not go directly to college because he needed a year of high school credits. So he would attend high school in Mexia while Aunt Verna managed our house and cared for Mother until she was accepted at the sanitorium. Then they would live with us for the six months she would have to be away.

Until this time I had hoped we would move to San Angelo to be near Mother, but my very persuasive mother convinced me that we needed to stay right here because Daddy had a good job and I had a good school and she would feel happier knowing that Aunt Verna was taking care of us.

Aunt Verna, Aunt Della and Aunt Ira were busy making robes, nightgowns and other clothing to fill the new trunk Daddy had bought for mother. Word soon came that the sanitorium would have a room for her in early February. I prayed that the day would never come, but it came.

Mother looked beautiful the day she left. Her long auburn hair was coiled low on her neck in a figure eight and her belted brown coat reached almost to the top of her dainty hightop shoes. A matching brown wool hat was perched above the sparkling brown eyes. She had gained a few pounds with Aunt Verna's good care, making her face a little fuller and her color more natural.

Daddy and I had promised each other not to cry when she left so as not to upset her. We took her aboard the train, kissed her despite germs and doctor's orders, and Daddy opened the train window so she could wave to us on the platform.

"Take care of each other . . . get some sleep, John . . . and don't work too hard . . . study hard, Babe, and make some good grades . . . write to me every night." Mother kept calling messages and waving until the train went out of sight. We watched with tears flowing freely. When we reached the car I could not stop crying. I'd been brave and cheerful long enough. Now I was desolate, hurt, frustrated and angry.

"Daddy," I sobbed, "I'm mad because God didn't answer my prayer."

"What prayer, Hon?"

"My Sunday School teacher said God answers our prayers but I asked Him to make Mother well before she had to go away—and He didn't."

My father had picked up the crank for our usual car-starting ritual, but he put it down and slid into the seat beside me. "Well, now," he began, "you see, Poochie, God's a lot smarter than we are. He knows that an old gang pusher like me and a schoolkid like you can't cure TB, so he gave us doctors and taught them how to do the job."

"Does God talk to doctors?"

"Not the way I talk to you, I guess, but he helps them learn how to do their jobs just like he helped me learn how to pull wells and helped you learn to read."

"But why does it take so long?"

"Well, Honey, six months won't seem so long if we keep busy. I'll take you on to school now, and I'll go to work, and we'll both be too busy to worry."

Aunt Verna cooked a special dinner that night and announced to us at the table, "We are all going to stay busy and happy and live like a normal family. Who wants to dry dishes for me?"

"I will," I volunteered.

"And who wants to sweep the porch and burn the trash?"

"I'll do that, Fatty," Uncle Burney responded. I always giggled when he called her Fatty, for she was a tall, willowy woman without an ounce of fat on her body. The reason he gave for calling her Fatty was "because she isn't."

Then Aunt Verna pointed her finger at my father and continued, "And you, little brother, are going to take a bath and get a full night's sleep. I have three kettles of water ready to pour in that tub."

"I'll use them just as soon as I write Vina a letter," he said, and, beginning that night, he wrote her a letter every night and received one from her every day they were apart. He lived for those letters and kept them in his trunk tray until it was too full for the lid to close.

Wortham, Texas
FEBRUARY—MAY 1925

WE HAD BARELY SETTLED IN after Mother's departure when my father was transferred to the Wortham field. Wortham was a small town about eight miles north of Mexia. The oil field stretched between the towns. We rented a farmhouse with two large bedrooms and a shed-room for cooking and eating. We actually lived a little nearer to Mexia than to Wortham. Uncle Burney could continue to drive to the Mexia school, but I would have to transfer to an elementary school in Mexia. Giving up Forest Glade School and the friends and classmates I had kept for almost two years, along with my adored Miss Unger, was traumatic for me. Even the Bumgardners and McCroreys were too far away for frequent visits.

I rode to school with Uncle Burney in a stripped-down Ford he had bought which we called the hoopie. He laughed and joked all the way each day, telling me jokes and funny stories. I could not remain despondent in his company.

Since he was an adult attending classes with teenage students, he must have had trying situations of his own, but I never knew about them. In retrospect, I know he was just helping a little girl over a rugged time in her life. It was not the last help I would receive from this cowboy-turned-educator and his gentle wife.

My teachers in Mexia must have been adequate, for I made acceptable grades, but I cannot remember a single teacher's name. Perhaps some psychological block prevented me from relating to them for fear of being hurt by another parting.

The happiest time of day for me was about 7:00 P.M. when my father came home and gave me my part of the letter from Mother. I always went straight to answer it but could not pour out my problems to her. Aunt Verna kept reminding me that Mother would get well much quicker if I sent her only cheerful letters.

About this time Mother began sending me very unusual pieces of paper doll furniture. They were printed inside Cloverbloom butter cartons, and workers in the sanitorium kitchen saved them for Mother to send me. Heretofore I had pictured Mother in a far-away hospital with impersonal doctors and nurses, but this helped me to change that image. Perhaps the people out there in West Texas were normal, friendly people after all. I felt better about them caring for my mother.

Since I had no playmates near the Wortham farmhouse, I spent my leisure time playing in a fantasy world with my paper dolls. I could not control events in my own life, but trouble never marred the lives of my paper characters.

Realizing my need for companionship, Aunt Verna planned an Easter egg hunt in the yard of the farmhouse. Aunt Ira and Aunt Della helped with the party and brought their children to spend the day. Billie and I helped Dellon and Martha Jane fill their baskets. Dellon took one bite out of each egg and smeared his white rompers with rainbow colors. Martha Jane wanted only red eggs in her basket and threw all the others out. I laughed more that day than I had since Mother left.

Daddy was cheerful, too, for the sanitorium reported that Mother was making good progress and could now have some needed dental work done. The dental work proved quite expensive and took a large part of Daddy's savings. We all agreed to try to spend less money and to replace the savings as soon as possible.

At next report the dental work was completed, and Mother had almost reached the halfway mark in her treatment. The doctors recommended that she remain in a high, dry climate for at

A connection gang working for Boyd Oil Company in the Mexia-Wortham field in 1923. The gang pusher, center, wearing overalls, is my father.

least a year after her release from the sanitorium. Such a small report to bring about such an upheaval in a family!

"There is nothing to do," my father declared, "but go out there somewhere and get a job before she is released." As usual, he took things as they came.

"You can go right now, John," Uncle Burney suggested. "We'll keep Estha until you are settled and Vina is released."

"No. I want to go with you, Daddy," I said quickly.

"But you have to finish the school term, and you have no place to stay while your Daddy works," Aunt Verna explained.

"I'll talk to the men in the office tomorrow. Maybe they can give me a line on where to look for a job," my father said.

I was not happy with the way this conversation went, so I insisted, "I want to go wherever you go."

"We will decide all the details after I talk to the men about a job," he said. "Now, let's go write to Mother and tell her we will be moving out west to make a home for her."

The next afternoon he had good news. The company superintendant, Mr. Pearl, offered Daddy a letter of recommendation to Mr. Cromwell of the Texon Oil and Land Company out near Best, Texas. If Mr. Cromwell had no immediate openings, he would be sure to know of someone who was hiring at the time. Mr. Pearl also encouraged my father by telling him that, with his experience and good work record, he should be able to get a job anywhere he wanted one. This made him feel better about the move, but he knew he did not have enough money to make the trip and pay living expenses until he got his first paycheck on a new job. He would have to work another month and save every possible penny.

Almost every day for the next month one question was debated. Should I be left with Aunt Verna, Aunt Ira, Aunt Della or my grandmother, or should I go with my father? If my father drove away without me I was sure I would never see either of my parents again. Each discussion ended with me in tears.

On one of our now-infrequent visits to the Bumgardners I voiced my fears to Aunt Ira. "Why don't you just wait and see what your dad decides?" she asked quietly. "I don't think he has any idea of leaving you here."

"He doesn't?" This opinion surprised me. "How do you know that?"

"Well, has he ever asked you to stay? Who brings up the subject?"

I had to think about this for a while. "I guess it is usually me," I had to admit.

"I think if he was considering leaving you here he would be trying to prepare you for it," she reasoned. "At any rate, he will take you if he possibly can find a way to do it." She suggested that I not mention it again until he made his decision. How could I keep quiet when it meant so much to me?

As things happened my father did not have to make a decision. Neither did I because it was suddenly made for us by the next letter from Mother:

> *My Dearest Little Girl,*
>
> *I am so happy I could run up and down these halls and shout, because I am going to see you and Daddy. My friends are anxious to see you too, for I have talked about you so much and shown them your pictures.*
>
> *Ask Aunt Verna to buy you one new dress to wear when you come by here on your way west. Nothing expensive, just so it looks nice and you have not outgrown it.*
>
> *I am counting the days!*
>
> *Mother*

It had not occurred to me that a visit to Mother would be part of the trip. I held my breath as I handed the letter to Daddy. He passed it on to Aunt Verna, and she read it quickly. A big smile lit her face, and she said, "We'd better dress this young lady up so her mother will be proud of her."

My three aunts got together and made me a red silk dress with small white figures and plenty of ruffles. Aunt Verna bought me a pair of patent leather slippers with a strap across the instep. Daddy bought me three pairs of striped denim coveralls and a pair of sandals to wear on the trip. He also bought himself a new shirt and tie to wear when we went to see Mother.

We stored several large trunks and boxes with the Bumgardners, for they were to follow us a little later if jobs were plentiful out west. Our few pieces of furniture were stored in the barn at McCrorey's dairy. "We'll come back and get them someday," Daddy said.

We took only three suitcases, including a new metal one containing Daddy's dress suit and the nightgowns for Mother. Daddy's greasy workboots stood on the back floorboard along with the chuckbox of food and supplies to be used eating out at the side of the road or in tourist courts. A few quilts, sheets and pillows completed our load except for the goodies my aunts sent along for us to eat and the supplies we carried on the running boards down each side of the car. Extra tires, tubes, tools, jugs of water and other supplies were tied securely and covered with pieces of canvas wagon sheet.

Early on the morning of our departure the men finished storing our furniture, and we said goodbye to the McCroreys, heading the little car to the west. A few miles out of town I looked back and remarked, "There's a big fire back there somewhere." Daddy looked over his shoulder. "Looks like someone is burning trash or old oil." We didn't look back again. We were on our way to see Mother, and we hadn't seen her in four long months. My father sang and whistled all the way.

The Road West

MY FATHER WAS DRIVING a Star touring car with open sides and a black top made of waterproofed material. It was about two hundred miles to my Aunt Lillie Barker's ranch house in Mason County, near Brady. We planned to stay overnight with her.

Roads were mostly two-lane dirt thoroughfares, and the little car could make about twenty-five miles an hour at best. It was a long hard day of driving and only a short stop for lunch, so I fell asleep in the late afternoon.

It was dark when I woke. We were driving down a narrow country lane with trees arched overhead. The car lights seemed to shine down a long green tunnel.

"Are we nearly there?" I asked sleepily.

"Just five or ten minutes more," my father answered. "We'll ford Brady Creek, and then the road leads right up to their backyard."

"What's 'ford'?" I wanted to know.

"It's when you drive across shallow water where it runs on gravel or rocks."

"Oh." I had hardly uttered this confirmation of understanding when the car lights shone across what seemed to me a frightening expanse of water. I was glad to know it was shallow.

We drove into the water. Sure enough, it seemed shallow at first. Then, as we drove, it became deeper, and suddenly the car was sinking. The lights glowed under water until the engine stopped.

My father turned his back to me and barked, "Get on my back quick and hold tight!" I obeyed immediately.

The water was deep and dark when he stepped off the toolbox on the fender and began to swim toward the creek bank with me clinging to his back. He swam only a few strokes until he was able to start wading. When he waded out on the bank, I slid to the ground. I looked back and just the top of the car was showing, as if it floated on the water.

The moon emerged from behind a cloud and lit a silver path along the creek. Our eyes followed the path and upstream, not more than a quarter mile, we could see a new iron bridge spanning the creek.

"I'll be dadgum," said my dad, "they've deepened the channel and built a bridge since I was here."

We trudged up the hill in squishy shoes. The house was dark, so we woke the family. Daddy and Uncle Henry took a team of mules and pulled the car into the backyard, water still pouring from it.

"My pretty clothes," I cried. "How can I go see Mother with no new dress?" Aunt Lillie assured me that I would have a pretty dress if she had to make one herself.

Aunt Lillie, Mother's older sister, had been married to Uncle Henry two years before Grandmother Bumgardner died and left my mother the oldest at home. The Barkers always lived on a ranch, for Uncle Henry was a man who communed with horses better than with people. He had the manner and bearing of a cowboy but his peaceful, unlined face was not typical of an outdoorsman.

Aunt Lillie, a short, thick-set little woman with graying hair gathered in a bun low on her neck, always wore flat slippers and a figured cotton housedress covered with a starched apron on which she constantly wiped her hands.

The Barkers had two teen-age children, Abbie, who was a younger version of her mother, and Belvery, a tall bony boy with a smiling face somewhat like his father's. The two children rode horses a long distance to a one-room school on a neighboring ranch. Since we were the first three Bumgardner grandchildren, and they were several years older than I, they seemed to enjoy catering to me. Spoiling me was what my mother called it, but I loved it.

Belvery left his bed that night to help the men with the car and the mules, while his sister hurried to show me a doll and a box full of doll clothes that she had made for me. This took my mind off the car and its contents. I slept with Abbie and my new doll that night.

Next morning when I finally woke, the Barkers' clothesline and fences were full of our belongings. Aunt Lillie and Abbie were working with our clothes.

"Look!" Abbie greeted me. She had just finished pressing my red silk dress but wanted me to try it on to make sure it hadn't shrunk. It fit fine, but my shiny new slippers had shriveled and shrunk to half their size.

Fortunately, the new metal suitcase had been almost water-tight. Daddy's suit could be saved by the tailor shop in town. His dress shoes, like mine, were ruined. "But his old greasy boots," Aunt Lillie declared disgustedly, "just shed the water like a duck's back."

The fried chicken and all other goodies prepared by my aunts back in Mexia were in an unappetizing condition, but all these things were of small consideration compared to the car. Could it be fixed? If not, how could we go on? We didn't have money for a new car.

My father and a mechanic in town worked on the car for three full days. They took the motor apart, cleaned it and put it back together. About dusk on the third day a happy and smiling John Briscoe drove into the yard in the little car. When he stopped to open the gate, Uncle Henry said in his soft voice, "She's running like a Big Ben alarm clock."

By this time all our clothes had been washed, ironed and re-packed. Aunt Lillie packed our chuckbox, adding a packet of biscuits, a bowl of homemade butter and a jar of jam.

Next morning we left the ranch about sunrise. The Barkers kept waving and calling, "Don't drive in any more creeks!" We were happy to be on our way again.

The repair work on the car, two pairs of new shoes and two cheap suitcases had taken too much of our money. We would have to be careful until we were sure Daddy had a job. We agreed that it would be best not to tell Mother about Brady Creek, not just yet anyway.

In San Angelo we rented a tourist cabin, changed our clothes and drove out to Sanitorium, Texas. It was not at all like a hospital. Sanitorium was a little city all its own with dozens of white buildings, many of them with sleeping porches for the patients. There were sidewalks, curbs, grass and flowers. People walked about as if they enjoyed being there, and none of them looked sick to me. I loved to hear the nurses walk by, for their starched uniforms rustled importantly.

We were shown into a large living room where small groups of people carried on conversations seemingly oblivious to other groups. Then my mother came down the wide staircase.

I had known no joy in my short life equal to that of seeing my mother for the first time in four months. She looked beautiful but so different! They had asked her to cut her long hair, because caring for it tired her arms too much. She was wearing a bob almost as short as my Buster Brown. Suddenly I forgot all the words I ever knew. I was speechless.

Daddy wasn't speechless. He kept repeating over and over, "You look so well. You don't look a bit sick. You look well and healthy!" That's when I began to feel sure that my mother really would be well again.

Soon we were laughing and hugging each other. We met all

Mother at the sanitorium with her
hair cut for the first and only time.

of Mother's friends, even the kitchen workers who had saved butter cartons for me. We strolled over the grounds with Mother as
our guide. We sat on the benches that were scattered about the
grounds and told her how good it was to see her and hear her voice
again. I even did a few cartwheels on the beautiful green lawn just
because one of Mother's nurses asked me to.

Mother was allowed visitors from 1:00 to 3:00 P.M. and from
7:00 to 8:00 P.M. on Saturdays and Sundays. There were no
weekday visitation hours without special permission. We visited
her Saturday, spent the night in our tourist cabin and went back
twice on Sunday. Our leavetaking was full of hope this time, for
we would be together again in two months. We promised to write

her the minute we had seen Mr. Cromwell about the job. She kissed us goodbye and started up the stairs, for her naptime bell had sounded. We watched until she was out of sight, then walked slowly to the car.

As we left the little city we congratulated ourselves—neither of us had mentioned Brady Creek. Daddy was not sleepy, so he thought we might drive a little while before we got a tourist cabin for the night.

The road was almost deserted, so we stopped about dusk and changed our clothes. I put on a pair of striped coveralls, and Daddy dressed himself in his customary suit of khakis. We carefully folded our "dress-up" clothes and packed them away. He spread a quilt on the back seat for me.

"Now, if you get sleepy, you can climb over the seat and take a nap while I drive."

After dark there was nothing to see except the beams of the headlights down the road, the stars in a cloudless sky and the glimmer of a half-moon on a treeless landscape. I soon climbed over into the back seat and fell asleep listening to my father's whistling as he drove.

When I opened my eyes, it was daylight, the car was still and my father was missing from the front seat. I sat up quickly, a panicky feeling in my throat. There he was in front of the car. His face was covered with lather, and he was squinting into a small mirror he had leaned against a wash basin on the hood of the car. He was scraping away shaving lather with a straight razor.

I looked for my sandals, found them on my feet, climbed over the door onto the loaded running board and then jumped to the ground. "Daddy, why did we sleep in the car?" I asked.

He twisted his mouth to one side to get at the whiskers on his neck. "I just drove until I got sleepy, and there wasn't a tourist court anywhere around here. We saved three dollars, too. That may come in handy on down the line."

"Why didn't you let me sleep in the front? The back seat is bigger."

"Well, I can't stretch out in either seat so one is as good as the other for me."

I felt there was a flaw in his reasoning somewhere but I could not point it out, so I let the subject go. "How much money do we have left?"

"About twenty-five dollars. I had to pay some bills for Mother and leave her a little spending money."

"Is twenty-five enough?"

"Yeah, it's a good bit. It will last if I get a job right away."

"Are we going to eat breakfast here?"

"Yes. I heated a little water to shave, but my fire's out. How about finding some more wood?"

I took a quick look around. The ground was flat in every direction. Not a tree, house or hill broke the landscape. Small scrubby bushes grew in clumps here and there over the hard-packed earth, but their branches were no bigger than toothpicks. Far to my left I could see a wooden derrick, the only object tall enough to pierce the horizon.

"Where am I gonna get wood?" I asked helplessly.

"Just pick up those little greasewood sticks," he directed. "They burn pretty good."

The greasewood made a hot fire alright, but it took a lot of sticks to fry eggs and bacon. Daddy pulled out a small blackened pot and made himself some coffee but gave me a cup of condensed milk diluted with water.

After breakfast I poked a hole in an orange so I could suck the juice out. Then I began turning the rind inside-out in order to eat the orange.

"That's messy," my Daddy remarked. "Why don't you cut it in little squares like Mother does?"

"I don't know how she does it. Do you?"

"No. You'll just have to go ahead and eat it like a pig. We may both grow snouts before Mother gets home."

I liked this joke a lot, so we both laughed and laughed. Then we put our dirty dishes back into the chuckbox because there was not enough water left in the jug on the running board to wash them. We put out the fire before pulling back on the road.

"Will we get there today?" I asked.

"Yes. We're between Barnhart and Big Lake. We should get to Santa Rita before noon if we have no trouble."

I worried a lot about more trouble since the incident at Brady Creek. As we rode along I watched the road ahead carefully. When I saw what appeared to be water up ahead I asked, "If we come to some more water in the road, we're not going to drive through it, are we?"

"Gosh, no," my father assured me, "but there won't be any water on this road."

"But I see a lake or something up there."

"Oh, that's just a mirage," he explained. "That's a funny reflection the sun makes. It just looks like water."

I was skeptical, but since we never reached the water on the road, I had to believe it was true.

We drove through the towns of Big Lake and Best, then followed the Orient railroad tracks for a few miles and turned left across the tracks to Santa Rita.

Santa Rita Summer
1925

SANTA RITA NO. 1, the discovery well of this field, was named for the patron saint of the impossible. It was the neatest and cleanest such oil camp I have ever seen, more like a city than a camp.

There were no tents or shacks, and no trash was to be seen. The streets were wide, bladed smooth and heavily oiled to keep down dust. All the houses seemed new and were built in perfect city blocks. Concrete sidewalks, fresh and new, outlined each block.

We drove to the company headquarters building and parked. I chose to stay in the car while my father took his letter of recommendation and went looking for Mr. Cromwell.

I glanced about, mentally labeling the different buildings. Across from the office stood the company mess hall. To the left of it marched rows of two-room boxcar houses with porches front and back. These, no doubt, housed the field workers' families. The larger houses with four rooms and two wide porches would be the homes of office and management workers. The big house, with at least five rooms and a front porch decorated with a trellis and a porch swing, could only be the home of the farm boss. In this case, that was Carl Cromwell.

I identified the light plant, the apartment houses, the men's bunkhouse and a toolhouse. A small building near the railroad tracks would be the train station. Across the tracks and back the way we had come was a rather large grocery store with a gasoline pump out front.

The office where my father met Mr. Carl Cromwell, gave him his letter of recommendation, and was hired while I cartwheeled along the new sidewalk in front of the building. Abell-Hanger Foundation Collection, Samuel D. Myres Photographic Collection. Courtesy the Petroleum Museum, Midland, Texas.

Dotted over the landscape in every direction stood the familiar gridwork of wooden oil derricks with their long belt houses, each ending in a square engine house. The walking beams moved up and down rhythmically. The familiar slush pits, bull wheels, boilers and batteries of tanks were visible, too. It looked like every oil field I had ever seen except for the tall torches that burned all over the field. I would learn later that the natural gas in this field came from the ground in a poisonous form and had to be piped into the air and burned day and night because of its danger to man or animal. That day, however, I thought they had more street lights than they really needed, and I wondered whose job it was to put them out and re-light them morning and evening.

The memorial to the Santa Rita No. 1 on the grounds of the University of Texas at Austin. Abell-Hanger Foundation Collection, Samuel D. Myres Photographic Records. Courtesy the Petroleum Museum, Midland, Texas.

This appraisal of my surroundings took less than five minutes. I had been riding since daybreak, so I got out a small mirror and comb, parted my hair in the middle and smoothed it into place. Then I climbed over the car door and jumped to the ground. Aware that I must act the proper young lady, waiting for her father, I tripped sedately along the sidewalk. But the sidewalk was so smooth and white that when I reached the corner I threw decorum to the winds, swung my feet in the air and cartwheeled the full length of that beautiful walk.

I was back in the car recombing my hair when my father came out of the building. I could tell by the purposeful way his heels struck the pavement that he had the job.

"That job was mine all the time," he began. "Mr. Pearl had written Mr. Cromwell a letter, and he had been expecting me for three days."

"How much money?" I asked gleefully.

"Five dollars a day, and I start right now."

"Right now?"

"Yes." He turned and pointed to a rig about half a mile away, near the point of a small hill. "See that rig?"

"The one with the rods and tubing in the derrick?"

"That's the one. Cromwell drilled it himself, and he wants me to get it back on the beam by night if possible."

"All by yourself?"

"No. He has a couple of boll-weevils and one roustabout that worked a few days." A boll-weevil in roustabout lingo meant a rank beginner.

"If I park by the rig will you play in the car while I work?" he asked.

"Sure. I'll watch you work."

"But you can't come near the derrick."

"I know that."

"Then let's go to the store and get some cheese and crackers for lunch. We'll mail a card to Mother so it will leave on the evening train."

By 1:00 P.M. my dad had the engine on Santa Rita No. 1 running full throttle, and the men had gone to work. I watched for a while, then took my jacks and ball to the shady side of the car, turned a metal suitcase down flat and sat on the ground to play a game of jacks.

If my hard rubber ball could have transformed itself into one of crystal, capable of spanning four decades, I might have seen myself far in the future, a wife, mother, teacher, writer, tourist, standing on the edge of the campus of the University of Texas in

Austin, viewing this same rig through a camera lens and reading the inscription on a marker there:

> Santa Rita No. 1 was drilled by Texon Oil and Land Co. using the rig which now stands here. The drilling location was in the Permian Basin near Big Lake, Texas. Drilling operations, nearly abandoned at times, covered twenty months before the well came in on May 28, 1923, at 3055 feet.

My ball had no prophetic properties It remained hard rubber, and I had no vision of the future.

By seven o'clock that evening the walking beam on No. 1 was nodding to the rhythmical "putt-putt" of the engine and my dirty, greasy, tired but happy father was suggesting a meal at the mess hall before we went to the bunkhouse to sleep.

"I'm gonna sleep in the men's bunkhouse?" I couldn't believe what I was hearing.

"That's all they have right now. We'll get a company house as soon as one is available."

Only a few men lived in the bunkhouse at this time, so we took two cots at the far end of the long room. My dad and one of the men put an army-blanket curtain over the shower room for my convenience, and the men called me "Little Roustabout" and gave me nickels for ice cream or candy.

When Daddy and I were all cleaned up we put our dishes in the shower, scrubbed them with Lava soap and dried them on one of Daddy's clean undershirts. The two army cots we occupied that night felt better than any cot has a right to feel.

This sleeping arrangement continued for several nights until my father discovered an unused toolshed near Santa Rita No. 1. The floor was grimy from its use during the drilling operation,

The Santa Rita No. 2, showing the boiler, a flow tank, and the tool shed my father and I lived in until Mother came home. Carlene Cromwell Peavy Collection. Courtesy the Petroleum Museum, Midland, Texas.

but he was told we could use it while we waited for a house, so we scrubbed it out and moved in.

The toolshed was barely big enough to hold the few pieces of furniture we bought—two new mattresses, a second-hand bedstead, an army cot and a beat-up kerosene cookstove. We added a large box that served as a table, desk, chair or cabinet, whichever was needed. We called it the baby grand piano because it did everything but play tunes.

We rose at five each morning, cooked enough biscuits to last all day (my father hated bakery bread), prepared our lunch and got to work by seven o'clock. He worked until 7:00 P.M., when we returned to the cabin, had supper, wrote a letter to Mother and fell in bed. My father attempted to hire a woman to keep me during the day while he worked but never found one that met his approval.

Oil field pump jacks and rod lines. On display at the Petroleum Museum, Midland, Texas. Photo by Dick Stowe.

All day long I amused myself by playing with my doll, reading whatever books or magazines I could get my hands on, writing letters or watching the work in progress at the rig my father happened to work on that day. I counted the cars on each passing train and spent a lot of time hanging upside down on rod lines.

Rod lines were used throughout the field to make one engine pump two or more wells. The metal rod, some two inches in diameter, passed through slots in the top of a line of posts about three feet tall. Each stroke moved the rod about two feet in one direction, then back, then forward again.

I could hold the rod with my hands, lift my feet and swing back and forth. Better still, I could hook both knees over the rod and ride upside down with my hair sweeping the alkali dirt as I moved to and fro.

My father objected to the latter position because it called for a shampoo each night, but since I preferred it, he took me to his barber and got me a boy haircut. After that, since I wore coveralls, everyone mistook me for a boy. When someone asked, "What's you name, son?" I quickly replied, "I'm not a son. I'm a girl."

One morning as I played near the car I saw an old man—he must have been at least forty—trudge up to the rig floor carrying a tool of some sort. He wore a clean khaki suit and a felt hat pulled low over his eyes. My father shook his hand, and they walked toward the car.

"Mr. Dugan, this is my little girl," my father began.

"I'm nine years old," I hastened to add, not too happy about being called "little."

"Her name is Estha," my dad continued. Then he turned to me. "Mr. Dugan runs the blacksmith shop." He pointed to a small building near the railroad.

Mr. Dugan solemnly shook hands with me and invited me to come with my dad to his shop sometime soon. He had a kind face and crinkled blue eyes which he kept squinted as if the light was too strong. I liked him immediately.

Dad and I became frequent visitors at the blacksmith shop. Mr. Dugan lived in a lean-to room behind the shop and was admittedly a lonely person. He insisted that I be his guest anytime my father needed a place for me to stay. This was a help to my dad, and I stayed with Mr. Dugan briefly many times. We often brought him some of our hot biscuits for his breakfast when we came to work in the morning.

Mr. Dugan had a few good books that he let me read, the most memorable being *David Copperfield*, which he helped me to read and understand. He also had stacks of scientific magazines and countless copies of a pulp magazine called *Western Action*. Neither Mr. Dugan nor my father seemed concerned about the contents of this reading material the way Mother had been, so I read them all. The technical ones were boring but I enjoyed the westerns.

I always took refuge with Mr. Dugan when a sandstorm blew in, for an open car was no protection from the stinging, wind-driven sand. Throughout July and August, the car served as my daily home. Mornings were fairly cool, but the car furnished little shade from the afternoon sun, so as soon as the sun tipped to the west, I played in the shadow of the derrick.

Standing about eighty feet tall, the broad derrick timbers furnished two long skinny shadows, with the crosstimbers making shady crossmarks in between. The timbers formed a focal point at the top of the derrick, where the shadows of the crown block made a little island of shade that moved steadily eastward as the sun dropped in the west. I learned to judge the hours of the afternoon by the position of the crown-block shadow. When the shadow reached as far as it would go before sundown, I put my toys and books in the car for the ride home.

I played, using my imagination, along the shadow of the derrick. At times I carried my doll and the long shadow became the road to Grandmother's house. If I rode a stick horse, it became the Santa Fe Trail. If I puffed along like a steam engine on the Orient Railroad, it was the railroad track bearing the train that would bring my mother home. If I high-kicked along the shadow in imaginary black tights and fishnet stockings, singing at the top of my voice, it was a vaudeville stage, and if I held an imaginary steering wheel in my hands, it was the long dusty road back to Mexia, to Forest Glade School, to all my friends and relatives.

I was lonely but not really unhappy with this life. I often yearned for a playmate, but Daddy had explained to me that we were saving money for the happy day when our family would be together again. We counted the days until the end of July.

The new company apartment house was almost finished with

an apartment reserved for us, and my father was looking for a better car to buy before Mother came home. Then came a report from the sanitorium. Mother would have to stay another month. I cried myself to sleep that night.

Next morning we parked beside Santa Rita No. 5, and as my dad climbed onto the rig floor there was a decided slump to his shoulders. He had a downcast look, which was unlike my father. Then I realized that I was not the only one who was disappointed. I felt very selfish, and I remembered Miss Unger's words, "You must always be an optimist."

I hoofed it over to Mr. Dugan's shop and spilled my troubles to him. He thought my dad needed a little change in his humdrum life. "The man works too hard, with no recreation," he said.

By the time my dad came to the car for lunch I already had a plan. "Daddy," I suggested, "let's go to a restaurant tonight and order tenderloin of trout."

He threw back his head and laughed. "On this desert? They never saw a fish out here!"

We settled for chicken-fried steak at a restaurant in Best. Then we stopped at a soda fountain for a strawberry ice cream soda, but the soda skeet at the fountain was promoting a brand new treat called "Eskimo Pie." It was a cake of ice cream coated with a chocolate shell. We loved it so much we each ate two.

Next we stopped in a jewelry store, at my father's suggestion, and picked out a little gift for Mother. It was a small gold brooch set with a jade center. Right in the center of the jade was a tiny seed pearl. It cost ten dollars, two whole days' wages for my father, but he hoped it might lighten her disappointment at having to stay another month. The lady at the store mailed it for us.

On the way home we dropped two letters in the mail, one to Mother and one I had written to the Bumgardners. After they were mailed I told my father what I had done.

"I wrote Uncle Buss and told him to come on out here be-

This wooden derrick, used in drilling, was left in place for pumping and servicing the producing well. On display at the Petroleum Museum, Midland, Texas. Photo by Dick Stowe.

cause there were plenty of jobs, and besides that, I wanted to see Dellon." My father laughed at my audacity but I assured him they would be here soon.

Two weeks later they arrived. Not really because of my letter, but rather, I think, because my uncle still felt a psychological need to make contact with the sister-mother figure in his life. They had visited Mother on their way to us. Their ultimate destination was New Mexico to investigate a business opportunity there.

Their truck was parked in front of our cabin, and they were sitting on our doorstep when we got home one evening. My uncle gave me a bear hug and said, "Well, bossy lady, you said 'come,' so we came."

And there was my own little Dellon, so big after all these months! He could walk and talk. He called me "Otta," which was close enough to Estha to please me. I couldn't kiss him enough or squeeze him enough. We both squealed and raised such a noise that Aunt Ira remarked, "You're going to wake the next county," but she was smiling.

My uncle's Ford truck was loaded with furniture but none of it was ours. They had brought the trunks and boxes we had left with them but our furniture had burned, along with the dairy barn, in the fire we saw behind us the day we left Mexia.

"Well, none of it was worth much except Vina's sewing machine," my father reasoned, "and I'll buy her a new one as soon as she is well." My father always expected tomorrow to be a brighter day.

The Bumgardners spent several days with us. The men took tarps and fashioned a tent on the side of our cabin just large enough to cover a bed that they unloaded from the truck. I spent the days at the cabin with Aunt Ira and Dellon during their visit. She washed my hair with coconut oil shampoo and rubbed Hinds Honey and Almond Cream into my arms and face. We opened the boxes they had brought to us, and she lowered the hem on a dress or two for me just in case I had to start to school before Mother came home.

Aunt Ira was vexed at the condition of our clothing. "Where did you wash these things?" she wanted to know, and when I answered, "The blowout box," she commented, "I thought so."

The blowout box was a wooden box built around a steam line opening where the men could place their work clothes to steam out the grease and grime. It was fine for heavy work clothes, but with constant use, it turned white underwear a dirty gray. She bleached and soaped the dingy garments but finally decided they were hopeless.

I lost no time worrying about dingy undies. I wanted her to talk to me about my mother. I wanted her repeated assurance that she would really come home in August.

"I don't think she really had a setback at all," Aunt Ira insisted. "I think they just wanted to be absolutely sure they didn't release her too soon."

The night before the Bumgardners left us we put a tablecloth on the baby grand piano and had a feast. I don't remember the food Aunt Ira cooked, but the tablecloth, good water glasses and matched flatware made it a special time.

After the Bumgardners left we climbed over trunks and boxes constantly. Some went under our beds, others were stacked in our way. We didn't worry about this because as soon as he traded cars Dad meant to take a day off to buy a few more pieces of furniture and move us into the new apartment.

Then Daddy decided to accept a pumping and switching job that became available, so our hours were changed. We now slept until 9:00 A.M. and had three free daylight hours before reporting to work at noon. Daddy worked until midnight, but it left me fewer waking hours to spend alone in the car.

The pump station was near Mr. Dugan's blacksmith shop. Dad worked in the station throughout his shift except for the time he spent gauging the tanks. I could never enter the engine room where large and dangerous engines ran constantly to pump oil. Nobody entered that room except authorized personnel.

Beside the engine room, however, was a small "dog house" that furnished a safe place to sit. A dog house was any little, built-on room. Some were used for crews to change clothes or store supplies. This one contained an old desk and a few beat-up chairs. We ate our lunch there, and I spent a lot of time there, but my father thought the best place for me to be while he was gauging tanks was right along with him, so I went along.

There were four batteries of tanks, two tanks in each battery, to store the oil pumped by this station. The tanks were gauged four times during a shift. The most distant battery, No. 3, was about half a mile from the station.

Each gauging job was completed in less than an hour. We walked to the battery, climbed the wooden steps to the top of the tanks, and I sat on the top step while my dad continued to the hatch or opening of each tank. He would throw open the hatch and run a little way down the catwalk—a broad walkway across the top of the tanks—to wait for the first rush of poison gas to be carried away by the air. When Dad considered it safe he would return, drop his weighted gauge-line into the tank and record the depth of the oil in the tank. He carried a handful of "waste" in his pocket to wipe the line clean after each use and always worked quickly to shorten his exposure to the gas. Waste was a by-product of cotton mills and was used for wiping hands and tools. When I heard the last hatch slam down, I knew it was time to start to the next battery.

For some reason battery No. 3 was the most dangerous. The gas seemed to hover longer there, and we were always glad when it was finished.

After we ate our supper and made the seven o'clock gauge I went to bed in the backseat of the car, but my father always woke me at eleven to go with him to gauge the last time. He jokingly said he was afraid to go alone, but I knew the real reason. He was afraid I might wake and stumble into the engine room looking for him. I must have slept quite soundly, though, for once I woke and found myself wearing a silver ring that Mr. Dugan had made and slipped on my finger while I slept.

After we made the last gauge, Charlie Waters would come to work the next shift, and we could go home. Mr. Waters was a tall, slender fellow with sandy hair. He and my father referred to themselves as Mutt and Jeff because of the difference in their heights. He was always giving me nickels and dimes for candy and ice cream cones. I could never eat all the goodies my father's friends provided funds for, so I saved the money in my stationery box.

One hot night a thunderstorm moved in just as we finished our shift. We hurried into the little car and headed for our cabin. It doesn't rain often in West Texas, but when it does, it is likely to make up for lost time. This was the first rain we had seen here, and it was coming down in sheets, driven by a strong west wind. The wind gusts drove the rain straight through the open car, and we ran into the cabin as fast as possible when we got there.

The cabin was little better than the car had been. The roof leaked in a hundred places. We soon had pots and pans all over both beds, trying to save the new mattresses. There was no place to lie down, and we couldn't have slept anyway because of the steady "ping, ping, pong" of the water in the pans. Finally we folded my cot against the driest wall and moved the big bed to the center of the room. Here we could both lie down, but soon big drops began to fall "splat" right on my father's forehead. I giggled and offered him my small umbrella which, to my surprise, he took.

He climbed on the bed, drove a nail in a rafter, and hung the umbrella upside down by the handle, letting the drops fall into the upturned umbrella. We both laughed because it worked, then fell asleep. The storm passed by quickly, and the next morning was sunny and bright.

When we started to work I found the doll Abbie had given me where I had left her in the car. She was a sodden clump of melted composition with no facial features at all. My father assured me that we would buy another doll right away. I wanted to find another doll to fit all those pretty doll clothes Abbie had made. I took the doll and put it behind the door as we hurried off to work.

My father related the experience to Charlie Waters that morning, and that kind man insisted on giving me three dollars to buy a new doll. I knew this was enough money to buy the prettiest doll in the Sears Roebuck catalog, so I hid it in my stationery box until I could borrow a catalog from someone. Then I forgot all about dolls in the excitement of a new car.

Our new car was not really new. It was two or three years old, but it was our first "closed" car. Almost nobody drove a touring car anymore. Ours was an Overland, a square black box on wheels. The back corners were slightly rounded, but the front was perfectly square with a sun visor that extended like a cap bill above the windshield. The engine was encased in a smaller square black box flanked on either side by rounded fenders. I almost wore out the cranks rolling the windows up and down.

The car had one more innovation. No cranking was required to get it started—it had a button to step on called a self-starter. Mother was sure to like that when she got home.

We had dreamed, yearned, planned and prayed for the day she would come home. When she actually came, we were not ready. The letter telling us when to meet her was delayed somehow. When we received it, about seven one evening, we learned that she would arrive at four the next afternoon. Charlie Waters told my dad not to worry—he knew someone would work tomorrow's shift. That solved one problem, but where to take her? There was no time to buy furniture and get moved, so Daddy asked a friend to bring a truck and help him move the big boxes to the apartment. Then we cleaned the cabin and cooked several of Mother's favorite foods, dressed ourselves in our unfamiliar "good clothes" and went to meet the train.

We waited—and waited—and waited. The train had a breakdown somewhere. Finally, at 8:00 P.M. it arrived, and the day I had looked forward to as the greatest day of my life turned into a nightmare.

Mother was so sick she had to be carried off the train directly to the infirmary. She and several other passengers had eaten sandwiches in a small restaurant while the train repairs were made. They all became ill a little while later. The nurse on duty at the infirmary called it a "touch of food poisoning" and gave her something to stop the cramps and vomiting. It was almost midnight when we finally took her to our cabin and she went to sleep.

Next morning my father went back to the train station to get Mother's trunk, but it had not been unloaded. He drove to Texon, three miles to the west, and found that it had been unloaded there.

I made coffee while he was gone, and Mother was feeling well enough to try drinking it. But when Daddy returned, he declared that she needed solid food and cooked a pot of oatmeal.

Suddenly my joy returned, and I kissed Mother on the forehead and said, "Oh, I'm so glad to have you home!"

At this she began to cry uncontrollably. "What did I do?" I asked. "What's the matter?" I was frightened.

As my father turned toward her from the stove, she cried "It's all my fault. The whole thing is my fault, and I feel so terrible—"

"What, Mother? What?"

"All this," she waved a hand around. "I made you do all this—"

By this time my dad had reached the side of the bed. "All of what?" he asked. "Tell us what's wrong."

She flung both hands wide and looked around the room.

"It's my fault that you've had to live in this . . . this hovel!" she gasped. "You had to spend every penny you made on me, and you're both half-starved, and burned up in the sun, and my little girl doesn't even have a doll—just that awful thing behind the door."

I turned quickly. When we closed the door last night, she had seen my doll. "Oh, no, Mother! It isn't like that. I left my doll out in the rain but Charlie Waters gave me money for a new one." Now I was crying, and Daddy was holding both Mother's hands and had a worried frown on his face.

"You didn't make us live here," I continued. "We found this place all by ourselves, and we fixed it up nice. We like this place . . . and our new mattresses and . . . and our baby grand piano."

"Your what?"

"That's what we call the box," my dad intervened. "We use it for everything . . . ." Our eyes turned to the box. It was topped with a bucket of water, a stack of dishes, my sandals, a drinking glass full of pencils, Dad's work gloves and a pot full of oatmeal.

The tears had not dried on Mother's face, but now she was laughing. "My crazy family!" she said as she swung her feet to the floor and reached for the robe hanging on the iron bedstead.

"Where are you going?" Daddy asked.

She tied the robe around her and lifted her chin in the perky gesture that we remembered well. "I'm going over to play the piano while you cook breakfast," she replied. This was the jaunty, vivacious mother I had expected to meet at the train yesterday. We were all smiling now—our family was together at last.

After breakfast Daddy opened his wallet, dug in the secret pocket and pulled out three bills. He smoothed them out and laid them beside Mother's plate. Her eyes widened as she took them in her hands.

"Three hundred dollars?"

"Yes," he answered, "we saved it because the rent on this 'hovel' is free, and I had more than that before I bought the car. This is for furniture, clothes and whatever we need to get us going."

"Did you trade the old car?" she asked.

"Yes, but it didn't bring much after the—after the two of us lived in it so long."

I caught my breath, but he hadn't said too much. We would tell her about Brady Creek, but not today.

"I've got money for a new doll, too." I showed her my treasures in the stationery box. Besides the three dollars from Mr. Waters, I had a handful of nickels and dimes given me by Daddy's generous friends. She promised to get a Sears Roebuck catalog and help me order a doll right away.

A battery of tanks with the stairs leading up to the "cat-walk."

Santa Rita
1925–1926

THREE DAYS AFTER MOTHER'S RETURN we moved into our new apartment. We put bedspreads on our beds, a tablecloth on our second-hand table and cushions on our second-hand chairs. Daddy and Mother went to the grocery while I stood on a box to arrange our dishes in the built-in cabinet above the sink where water, both hot and cold, ran at the turn of a faucet. We even had a small bathroom all our own.

There was a closet in the bedroom for hanging clothes, and Daddy had built legs for our packing box-dresser because it could not be nailed to the nice new walls. Mother and I loved the apartment, but Daddy said it was like living in a cracker box with other cracker boxes on each side. He had hoped for a house but did not complain when he was assigned an apartment instead.

I finished my work and went out back to put the packing paper in the garbage can. A group of children were playing tic-tac-toe on the sidewalk, and I stopped to watch for a minute. Nobody paid any attention to me until a girl about fourteen years old asked, "Did you just move into No. 4?"

"Yes," I answered.

"What's your name?" she asked.

"Estha Briscoe. What's yours?"

"None of your business!" she shouted as she moved away from the group. "I'm not gonna play with you, and they'd better not either." She pointed to the children who all were, by this time, listening.

"Why?" I asked. I had never seen any of these children before and couldn't imagine how I had offended them.

"Because your mother's got TB, and we don't want to take it."

"No, she hasn't," I corrected her. "She had it, but she is well now."

"She is not," the girl shouted. "My momma said nobody gets well with TB. They die! Your mother is gonna die!"

"No, No!" I was distressed. I wanted to set her straight, but she shouted, "Yes she is! Yes she is!" It was a good chant, so all the children joined in. I could not make myself heard, so I ran into the apartment and closed the door. I could still hear them chanting, "Yes she is!"

I didn't want Mother to know about this, so I took my dad aside and asked him what to do. He gritted his teeth and shook his head, then finally said, "Don't do anything. I'll talk to Mr. Cromwell tomorrow before I go to work. I was afraid somebody would be afraid to live near her."

Mother was instructed to stay in bed two hours each morning and two each afternoon, so when she lay down at 10:00 A.M. Daddy said, "You'd better go with me. Mr. Cromwell might want to ask you some questions."

We had heard that Mr. Cromwell, called Big Swede, was somewhat explosive when things did not please him. This time he hit the ceiling. After he'd exhausted his supply of expletives, all of which I had heard before, he apologized to me.

"I'm sorry, little girl, but I've got a little girl of my own, and if a kid treated her that way, I'd lose my temper." Then he turned to Dad.

"They gave you an apartment? I told them to give you a house. Why didn't you tell me?"

"Well—I didn't know what you had ordered or who made the assignments."

The boss barely heard him. "Ed! Come in here," he called.

A young man wearing a khaki suit and a bow tie hurried in.

"Ed," he repeated, "I put in an order for a house for Briscoe.

They gave him an apartment. Find him a house."

"But, sir," Ed began, "there are no empty houses."

"Then EMPTY one! Who's in No. 2 across from my house?"

Ed disappeared into the adjoining office and returned with a list in his hand. "Someone named Balfour. He just went to work last week."

"Last week? Briscoe's been here three months. Tell him he can have one of the new apartments with private bath, and move him out—today!"

"But, sir, he's in the field with the roustabout gang."

"Send someone after him, and send him to me. That private bath ought to convince his wife."

When we returned to the apartment Mother was already up. "You didn't rest two hours," Daddy accused.

"Where did you two go? I had a visitor who gave me some interesting news."

"Oh, oh," I said. I could see that my dad was building up to an explosion to rival Mr. Cromwell's.

"Did some catty woman come in here and—"

"No, no," she assured him. "She was a lovely lady, a Mrs. Young. She told me what happened yesterday. Two of her children were out there, and she brought them over to apologize. It seems there is a woman here who is afraid of me. They told us at the 'San' to expect some of that, so I sent her a little pamphlet along with assurance that I, and my family, would stay completely away from anyone who felt uncomfortable around us."

"But we're gonna move anyway!" I couldn't contain the news any longer. "We went to see Mr. Cromwell, and he cussed just like Uncle Buss, and then he gave us a house."

The house was diagonally across the street from the farm boss's house. It was exactly like the apartment but with larger rooms and no bath.

Large bath houses for men and women stood behind the row

of dwellings. They held showers, lavatories and huge water commodes with chains that hung down from tanks near the ceiling. The seats stood in the air at a forty-five-degree angle until pushed down by a person's weight. I was deathly afraid of this appliance, for my weight was hardly sufficient to hold the seat down even after I succeeded in pushing down and pulling up on all the right clothing in order to sit on it. My feet dangled a foot off the floor, and I was obliged to jump down, knowing that the seat would fly into the air as the thing flushed with a growl like a lion swallowing its prey. I felt sure that, someday, the thing would gobble me up and nobody would ever know what happened to me. My father soon built a small wooden platform to place in front of the appliance for all the little girls to use. This helped me tame the frightful monster.

My mother, always germ-conscious, worked out an exchange with the neighbors, and they took turns applying disinfectant to everything in the bathrooms, including floors and shower stalls.

After the move was completed we worked out a four-hour-a-day rest schedule for Mother, and my father was ready to go back to his job. It took some strong persuasion to convince me that he could handle the switching and gauging job without my help but, since the pump station was less than half a mile away, I had to content myself with daily visits to check on my father and Mr. Dugan.

Mother was anxious for us to get back to church, so Daddy and Charlie Waters arranged a trade-out, giving each man every other Sunday morning free. We drove to the First Baptist Church in Big Lake for our first service.

Our name reminded the minister of a colleague of his, the Reverend Billy Briscoe, my father's uncle. Learning of this relationship probably prompted the minister to call on Brother John Briscoe to lead the closing prayer.

I had never heard my father pray publicly before, but when he gave thanks for "all the great blessings we have so recently received," I wanted to shout "Amen!" But I wasn't a deacon, and so far as I could tell only deacons did that.

There were countless changes made around our house once Mother was home. The table was always set with a tablecloth and three full place settings. Food was served from bowls, not cooking pots. We had forgotten how good Mother's fried chicken and gravy tasted. The first time she made pot roast with vegetables and cornbread muffins, Daddy said "I hope I never see another can of pork and beans or sardines in this life or the next." Once again, pies and cakes appeared on our table and a pot of coffee waited for neighbors to drop in.

We even looked better now. My coveralls disappeared, and I wore new cotton dresses. A sewing machine had appeared from somewhere, and once again ruffled curtains danced in the breeze at all our windows. Daddy even wore a clean suit of work clothes every morning.

Our new neighbors were evidently not afraid of "catching the bug," for they helped us move in and the adults were on a first-name basis before the first night. Neighbors to the north of us were Clarence and Esther Stewart and a chubby nine-month-old called Sonny Boy. Sonny and his blond, blue-eyed mother had such fair skin that the West Texas sun kept them blistered and peeling constantly.

South of us lived Clarence's brother Dick and his petite and dainty wife, Lula. The Stewart brothers, both lean outdoor types, played and sang cowboy songs, music that would later be called Country and Western. We all gathered around in the evenings to sing along with them. I was fascinated with a sad and lonely song called "Little Joe, the Wrangler."

In a house on the south side of our block lived the Butlers, a young couple with a perky three-year-old named Margaret Eva. I was always asking her, "Where does your grandmother live?" I knew she lived in Mineral Wells, but it was fun to hear the little tyke say "Mimmy Wewws."

All these people became our Santa Rita family. We could share meals often, go on short trips together, keep each other's children, care for illnesses and share each other's joys or misfortunes.

There was also a young man, in his early twenties, who came to our house often. He liked Mother's cooking, and it was easy for him to drop by because he worked at the light plant just up the street from our house. Dad had met him before Mother came home, and the two developed a sort of father-son relationship. The young man, called Curly because of the mass of black curls that fell across his forehead, stood a head taller than my father but liked to confide in him concerning his ambitions and, more often, his problems.

Most of Curly's problems were of his own making. He liked a drink now and then, and, since liquor was illegal, he knew just where the nearest bootlegger could be found. Occasionally he failed to report for work and someone had to bail him out of jail. This embarrassed Curly, and he always promised, "I'll never do it again, but please don't tell my brother."

Curly's brother was a highly respected political figure back in his home county and was convinced that Curly had come out to the wicked oil fields and "gone to the dogs." My father said that Curly was just lonely and bored, with no friends his own age. Finally someone decided to put Curly on the evening shift, so he would be working during the hours he usually got into trouble. This plan seemed to work pretty well.

My father insisted that Curly drop by our house any time he chose. Dad, too, was working the evening shift and had a little time free in the mornings. I enjoyed the young man's company, too, and he seemed to like kids. He always had dimes in his pocket to pass out to the children as we played along the sidewalks.

One sunny day about a dozen children organized a parade. Wearing paper hats and beating pans with wooden spoons, we marched around every block in the camp. We were about to disband the parade and go on to something else when a skinny kid named Alex piped up, "Aw, I wanted to go up to the light plant and show Curly our parade." We decided to humor Alex, and Curly was delighted that we did.

"Why don't you parade over to the grocery store and buy ice cream?" he suggested as he fished dimes out of his pockets for all of us. We liked the idea until someone remembered we were not allowed to cross the railroad and the highway. Curly solved this problem. He asked his helper to take over for a while. Then, with Alex sitting astride his shoulders, he marched with us to the store and bought ice cream for everyone. His only stipulation was "Don't beat your pans inside the store."

A few days later, about eleven o'clock in the morning, we heard a loud noise coming from the company mess hall. Daddy and I were sitting on the front steps so we stood up and started in that direction. A dumpy, middle-aged woman ran out the mess hall door. She wore a large white apron and was shouting something about calling the police. Daddy and I went to meet her just as the door flew open again and a chair went flying into the street. "Come quick," she pleaded. "He's drunk."

"Who's drunk?" my dad asked.

"It's that Curly boy. He's wrecking the dining room."

"No, he's not drunk. He just walked by and talked to us a few minutes on his way to breakfast," declared my dad.

Again the screen door slammed back against the wall and the entire mess hall staff scurried out into the oiled street. Sounds of breaking dishes came from inside. My dad stepped to the porch and held the screen door shut with both hands in case there were more flying objects. "Come here, Curly," he called. The noise stopped. After a few seconds, Curly came to the door, a sheepish look on his face. "They tried to make me eat beans for breakfast," was all he said. He got there too late to make the eleven o'clock deadline, and a waitress refused his order for bacon and eggs.

"Well, Curly," my dad began, "come on down to my house, and Vincy will cook you some eggs."

The cook, his apron twisted sideways on his skinny body, was holding a cigarette paper in one shaking hand and trying to pour tobacco into it from a Bull Durham sack. "Eggs?" he asked. "He wants eggs? I'll cook him some eggs. Hell, he don't have to wreck the mess hall just to get eggs."

A chunky dishwasher, usually called a pearldiver, stood behind the cook, waving his water-wrinkled hands in the air and lamenting, "He threw my clean dishes in the slop bucket!"

Curly apologized for his temper fit and paid for the damage, but he kept begging my dad and Mr. Cromwell, "Please don't tell my brother." Curly later reported that he never had any more trouble getting eggs when he wanted them.

Mid-September arrived and it was time for school to start. There were about a dozen school-age children in the camp, so the company arranged for a bus from Best to pick us up for a four-or-five-mile ride to school there. I happily took my new lunch pail and joined the other children at the designated corner for the first day of school.

We were unloaded on the schoolground at Best, as were children from several other buses. Apparently nobody had bothered to count how many children would be brought in from surrounding oil fields. About 10:00 A.M., when I was finally sent into a fourth grade room, there was barely room to stand. But most of us stood, for more than an hour.

A teacher took our book cards and report cards and instructed us to put our names on our lunch pails and store them on a table in the back of the room. It was the last time I saw my cards, my lunch pail or the teacher.

A man came in and read off a list of names, mine among them, and said, "Follow me." We all walked like a line of ducks to a building about a block away where he led us into a room that was filled with students. This time I got to share a seat with another girl.

Soon another group of students filed in, making this room as overcrowded as the one before it. Another teacher came in and asked for our report cards and book cards. It took us a while to make her understand that our group had already given them to another teacher. She looked confused and left the room. That was the last time we saw her.

We waited and waited, the noise becoming louder all the time. Finally someone with a watch said, "It's twelve o'clock, and I'm gonna eat." Those who still had lunches ate them. We all migrated in and out to the water fountain and the outdoor toilets, but still no teacher came. Some of the children left and did not return. Some of the girls began crying.

It must have been 3:00 P.M. when a man came to the door with another of those lists in his hand. "These students come with me," he said. Then he read about twenty names. None of them were in the room. When nobody came forward, he asked, "Where is your teacher?" When nobody knew, he asked, "What is her name?" We didn't know that either, so he left.

Someone saw a schoolbus enter the grounds. A tall boy standing in the back called out, "Y'all can stay here if you want to but I'm gonna catch a bus and go home." We all left the building along with the boy. I decided to return to the place where I got off the bus that morning, and, seeing a few of the Santa Rita children in a group, I joined them.

We were all frightened, most of us were hungry, and nobody knew what to do. We clung together for comfort as one bus driver after another said, "No, I don't go to Santa Rita." When it became apparent that no more buses were coming, we sat on the steps of the school building. Someone suggested that we start walking, but nobody knew exactly which way to walk.

Now it was sundown, and all the girls were crying. The boys continued to scuffle and roughhouse. One little girl started walking toward the road, and we all begged her to come back. A boy named Arthur caught her by the arm and brought her back, saying, "Stay here, you silly girl. You'll get lost."

"I want to go home," she screamed.

"Alright!" he shouted back. "When my pa gets home at seven o'clock and I'm not there, he'll be over here raisin' hell all over the place. So sit still, and he'll take all of us home."

Why hadn't I thought of that? My mother was home. She'll come looking for me any time now, I silently told myself. Sure enough, pretty soon I saw our car, with Mother driving and looking relieved because she had found us. She squeezed all of us into the little car and drove home to the Texon office where a group of irate mothers had gathered. We never went back to school in Best.

Actually, we didn't go to school at all for several days. This suited me fine, for a package had arrived from Sears Roebuck with my new boy doll and a pair of roller skates. The doll was a cute little guy in overalls which I had chosen over the ruffled girl dolls in the catalogue. I named him Charlie Waters and promptly ran all the way to the pump station to show Mr. Waters his namesake. Then I buckled the skates on my feet and began learning to stand up on the things.

Skates were a must in Santa Rita. The perfect sidewalks around each block were finished with a smooth surface, not too good for walking in the rain. But then it scarcely ever rained in West Texas, and the kids skated every day.

I had never skated before, so my legs were soon skinned from knee to ankle; they grew thick scabs and then were skinned again, but I finally got the hang of it. Turning corners was tricky, but I mastered that also. My crowning achievement was the day I managed three cartwheels in a row while wearing roller skates. My mother threw up her hands and declared, "I'll never make a lady out of her!"

I was not in on the meetings held by the parents and the officers of Texon, but Mother came home with the news that we were going to have a school of our own in Santa Rita. Classes were to begin at Mrs. Arrington's house on the next Monday morning.

The Arringtons lived in one of the four-room houses furnished to white-collar workers, because Mr. Arrington held some sort of office job. The two front rooms were converted to schoolrooms. New desks and blackboards filled one room, while the other held recitation chairs, the victrola and shelves of fascinating new books. The company allowed Mrs. Arrington almost unlimited funds to make teaching and learning a joyful experience. Since there were only about a dozen children in the first seven grades, Mrs. Arrington taught all classes. Being an artist, she even gave us lessons in oil painting. I soon ranked her with Miss Unger, right at the top of the teaching profession.

I had more friends and playmates than I had ever hoped for—Louise Trice, Willie Reece Taylor, and several other girls and a few boys who lived in camp. We all skated together or played Tom Mix and Tony around the greasewood and catclaw bushes in the area bordering the camp. We could play as late as our parents would allow, for the torches made the entire area as light as day.

Then there were the babies. Loving Dellon had taught me to be fond of all babies. Since my parents loved little children too, we did a lot of babysitting for the small children in camp, all of it free of course.

Sonny Boy Stewart who lived next door was the youngest. He adored my mother and stayed with us often. My parents were an affectionate couple and might stop to exchange a hug or a kiss at any time. Sonny stopped all this by bursting into frightened tears each time it happened in his presence. We could never determine if he was jealous of his favorite babysitter, thought they were fighting or just wanted all the loving for himself.

Then there was Margaret Eva Butler, a cute blond between three and four years old. Her birthday was the Fourth of July, and we called her our little firecracker. Also there was Carlene Cromwell, the boss's little daughter who celebrated her fifth birthday while we lived in Santa Rita. Carlene's parents invited me to come over often to play dolls or eat supper with her. I did this on invitation only, for the Cromwells never allowed her to skate, ride stick horses, or march in parades with the older children. They did let her play at my house or spend a few hours with us while her mother went shopping.

Best of all, for the first time I had a "bosom pal." Her name was Geneva Loyce Smith. She had brown hair and eyes like mine, was only a little taller than me and wore a pair of tortoise-shell glasses that gave her a cute pixie look. She loved paper dolls, babies and Pollyanna books just like I did. She hated boys, arithmetic and moving, just like I did. We swore to be bosom pals "until we die."

Geneva Loyce was an only child too, when I first met her. Our mothers had become friends in the school meetings, and they remained so, even though Lucille Smith was a somewhat younger woman. The Smiths had recently moved to Santa Rita from Ranger.

Ranger was well known among Texas oil fields as the most rip-roaring nest of vice in United States oil field history. It was a small rural community when the discovery of oil suddenly exploded it to a 30,000 population. Law and order were never quite established, and the Smiths were glad to leave there for the quiet of Santa Rita where a whirlwind of desert dust, a rolling tumbleweed or a sandstorm was the most violent thing to be encountered.

Mrs. Smith and Geneva Loyce took a trip with Mother and

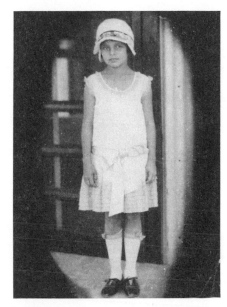

Sonny Boy Stewart, our little Santa Rita neighbor.

In Santa Rita at the age of ten I wore my Easter finery with fancy garters on top of my socks.

Birthday party for Carlene Cromwell, seated left. The arrow points to my best pal, Geneva Loyce Smith. I am standing second from right. The house in the left background is like the one I lived in.

me to Brady, Texas, to visit my Grandfather Bumgardner during a school holiday when our fathers had to work. Mother bought herself a pair of knickers for the trip and looked very fashionable in them until Grandfather Bumgardner remarked, "Is that all the clothes you brought?" Lucille Smith thought Mother should refuse to be intimidated, but Mother wore dresses the rest of the trip.

We visited with my grandfather and Granny Pearl, the lady my grandfather had married after his children left home. Granny Pearl's religion forbade her wearing makeup or any save the plainest of clothes. She wore her dark hair straight and knotted in a bun on the top of her head. Her skin had an olive tone, and her features were quite beautiful. She once saw me rubbing ointment on a rash in the palm of my hands and asked me to let her pray for my recovery. She held my hands in her own and said a short prayer. The rash disappeared in a few days, but I could never be sure if it was cured by ointment or prayer or just went away of its own accord.

Granny Pearl and my grandfather had two boys, both dark of complexion with black eyes and hair. Charlie was a year my senior, and Homer a year younger than I. I called them my little uncles but my mother always referred to them as "Papa's boys."

The boys and I took Geneva Loyce to visit the flour mill and then on to my grandfather's grocery store. He gave us candy and gum from the big glass case near his cash register. Geneva Loyce and I decided he must be a very important man, for his store was lined with forty-eight-pound sacks of flour decorated with his picture and his name in colorful letters. The picture on the flour bag showed him in a black suit with a dignified look on his face. In reality he always wore loose, rather rumpled clothes and he was a shy, complicated man who was never able to express his feelings. This may have stemmed from the fact that his parents had emigrated from Germany and only German had been spoken in his

home. In my young and inexperienced way I struggled to understand him.

Geneva Loyce thought I should kiss my grandfather, but I
was too much in awe of him. "I love him though," I assured her.
"I send him birthday cards and valentine cards every year." This
was true, but I was never sure whether he received them, for he
never mentioned them. I reasoned that such an important man
probably thought such things were childish, but I kept sending
them anyway. Years later, after his death, Granny Pearl found every one of them in his cash register drawer.

After our Brady visit we went to the country to see Aunt
Lillie and her family. My cousin, Abbie, had made me a paper
doll house out of cigar boxes. It was complete with papered
walls, hand-sewn curtains and hooked rugs. Geneva Loyce and I
squealed with delight at every detail, and the house gave me years
of pleasure. I guarded it carefully, and each time we moved it rode
beside me on the car seat.

We showed Mother where the car went into Brady Creek and
made jokes about the escapade, but she was not fooled about its
seriousness.

Belvery took Geneva Loyce and me to Brady Creek to fish
for crawdads. I caught one and mercilessly broke its pinchers off.
Belvery was showing my friend how to skip a rock on the water.

He had just given her a handful of flat stones when I presented
her with the disarmed crawdad.

Now Geneva Loyce had never fished for these creatures before. In fact, anything that wriggled or crawled frightened her, so
she flung both hands in the air, screamed and fled.

In flinging her hands, she let the stones fly every which way.
One hit me in the mouth, breaking the two huge top teeth that
had recently replaced my baby teeth. This did not end our friendship, however; in fact, it probably strengthened it, for she was
contrite and anxious to assure me that she had not thrown the

rocks at me on purpose. On the other hand, I felt a little guilty. I knew she was afraid of creepy-crawly things, and I was just a little too slow telling her I had broken the claws off just for her.

After we got home Mother took me to a traveling dentist who set up a temporary office in a Big Lake hotel room. I emerged with one dark tooth and a gold corner on the other. I wrote Geneva Loyce a little verse for her memory book that remains true to this day:

> I never will forget you
> I'm telling you the truth.
> Your name in golden letters
> Is stamped upon my tooth.

It was a happy time when the Bumgardners, fresh from New Mexico, came back to Santa Rita to visit us. They would be living nearby in Rankin, and I could see them often. I always felt happier when they were near.

The Christmas of 1925 is the brightest of my childhood Christmas memories. The previous Christmas had been sad because Mother was sick. This Christmas we were all together and well and more prosperous than we had ever been.

I had saved nickels and dimes until I had several dollars. Esther Stewart helped me order gifts from the catalogue for my parents. She took delivery on the package so I could surprise them. I ordered a garish leather purse with flowers embossed into the leather for my mother, and for Dad, I chose a round, tilting shaving mirror on a stand. It had holders for a soap bowl and shaving brush fitted to either side. I felt sure he had never owned such a treasure.

A week before Christmas my father took three days off work, and we drove to San Angelo to shop. We stayed in the Sealy House, so called because they featured Sealy mattresses. This in itself was a real Christmas treat, but there was more.

We drove our old boxy black Overland to the San Angelo

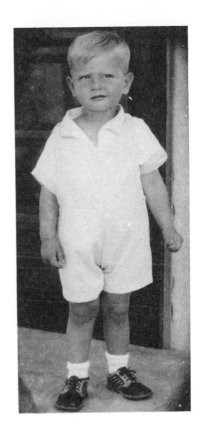

Dellon, age three, in Santa Rita. Dellon was an oil field kid who grew up to occupy a top management position in a major oil company.

Overland agency and let Mother pick the car she wanted in exchange. She picked a blue four-door sedan in the latest model, called "Red Bird." I enjoyed telling all my friends, "Daddy gave Mother a new Red Bird Overland, only it's blue."

Then we went to a haberdashery and bought Daddy a navy blue pin-striped suit. After that we shopped the town, and just before we returned for another night on those Sealys, we found a restaurant and ordered tenderloin of trout. Yes, I asked for a glass of milk, and no, they did not serve milk with fish.

Next morning we drove home, singing all the way. My father said, "This is the best Christmas we ever had, and we deserve it."

Mother and I agreed, but I kept eyeing the stack of boxes on the floor and in the seat beside me. One of them made a distinct "Ma-Ma" sound when I turned it over.

There were no Christmas trees in this desert country, and we did not wrap our gifts. I placed my parents' gifts on the foot of their bed on Christmas Eve. They found them just after supper and exhibited surprise and, I'm afraid, more admiration than they deserved.

Santa, whose identity I had learned in my first year of school, left my gifts beside my cot, and on Christmas morning I found a beautiful ruffly-dressed doll to keep Charlie Waters company. There was also a doll bed, a table and two chairs made by one of Daddy's carpenter friends. There were dishes, flatwear and a small cedar chest full of doll dresses made from the same fabric Mother had used for my own dresses. Since I was now ten years old my parents knew my playhouse days were numbered, so they supplied toys to prolong those days as long as possible.

One night in early February I woke a little past midnight. I had not heard my father's step on the porch. I looked out the kitchen window by my cot but could only see torches reflected in the window next door. I could hear Mother turning restlessly in the bedroom, and I knew she was wondering why he hadn't come home. I told myself Mr. Waters must have been late coming to relieve him, or a problem with some of the machinery required both men. I tried to sleep again, with no luck. Finally I heard a step on the walk, and someone climbed the two steps to the porch. It was not my father's step.

There was a knock at the door, and Mother called out "Just a minute" as she grabbed for her robe. I was beside her in my pajamas when she opened the door.

It was Mr. Dugan, and he began stammering in his soft voice. "Mrs. Briscoe,—could you come to the—the infirmary? John—

well, you see, he got too much gas, and Charlie and I took him there a little while ago."

"We'll be right there," Mother answered. I had already returned to the kitchen to get dressed.

The infirmary was two blocks away. Charlie Waters met us at the door. "I saw his lantern on the top of Battery 3. I think he fell down the steps," he said.

I rushed down the hall, ducked under the arm of the nurse at the door of the room and stood beside my father's bed. His eyes were open, but he was breathing hard. A doctor, probably from Big Lake, was placing his tools back in his black bag and giving the nurse instructions.

"Is he going to die?"

"And who is this?" The doctor turned to me, "No, he's going to be alright in a few days."

I turned back to the bed. My father's eyes were closed now but he lifted his arm, put his hand on top of my head and ruffled my hair with his fingers. Mother leaned over the bed and kissed his forehead.

He opened his eyes and said, "Tape—my tape."

Charlie Waters, standing behind Mother, answered, " I got your tape out of the tank, John. I have your lantern, too." Everyone turned as Mr. Cromwell entered the room, his pants and belt buckled over his pajama shirt and his bedroom slippers flapping on his heels. He looked at the doctor and asked, "Is he coming out of it?" Then, turning to Waters, he asked, "What happened?"

I had held my fear and anger as long as I could, so I blurted out, "It's that ole Battery 3—I told everybody I should keep going to work with him—can't you do something about those ole tanks?"

Mother rushed over, trying to shush me. This was the boss I was taking to task, the farm boss, the man who was becoming famous because he had drilled Santa Rita No. 1, the man whose word was law in Santa Rita.

Carl Cromwell understood me. I had played at his feet many hours with his own little girl. He patted me on the shoulder and replied softly, "I'm damned sure gonna try, honey!" He must have kept his promise because a few days later the pumpers were issued a mask of some sort to wear when gauging tanks. Charlie Waters pronounced them, "Not worth a sack of beans, but better than nothing—I guess."

When my father was able to talk he explained that the gas had been exceptionally bad that night. He ran for the stairs when he realized he'd breathed too much of it but blacked out just as he reached them. He had rolled all the way to the bottom where Waters found him. He went back to work in a week but developed a cough that lasted the rest of his life. Mother began urging him to find a job where there was no danger of poison gas.

Mr. Dugan had recently bought some lots in a new town forty miles west of us. Oil wells were coming in every day there and a boomtown was growing on the prairie. His property became part of downtown McCamey. After Mr. Dugan moved there to be near his business interests, he kept sending Dad messages to come to McCamey because opportunities were plentiful there. My father refused to leave until the school term was over. By that time the Bumgardners were in McCamey, and Uncle Buss wanted Daddy to come join him in a business he had started.

I felt sure I would die if I had to give up Geneva Loyce and all my other good friends. I couldn't bear to leave just as the new school building was being readied for the next school year. I related all these objections to my mother.

"I feel the same way you do, Babe," she replied. "We all love living here, and it is going to be hard to give up all these good friends, but I keep thinking how much harder it would be to live without our daddy."

Just the thought of life without my father was enough to quiet me. I choked back tears and agreed that we had to go.

It was hard to keep from crying the day we left, so as we rode along in the car I began reciting all the poems I had ever learned in school, beginning with the one by Rudyard Kipling I had learned in the first grade:

If you can keep your head when all about you

Are losing theirs . . .

I finished "If" and moved on to others. I was just finishing the Twenty-third Psalm when an arresting sight captured my attention. There, jutting up from the desert floor, was the first mountain I had ever seen. I stretched over the back of the front seat and pointed through the windshield. "Look, there's a mountain—that is a mountain, isn't it?"

"Sure is," my father replied.

I was fascinated. As mountains go, King Mountain, at 3100 feet, is nothing spectacular, but to me it was gigantic, reaching high above the desert with a flat mesa on top.

"Daddy," I asked, "what makes mountains?"

"Well," he answered hesitantly, "when God made the earth He had a lot of dirt and rocks left over so he stacked them up and called them mountains."

I would have accepted this explanation without question. After all, he had been right about God's plan to cure Mother, but Mother was smiling strangely. "Mother, is he teasing me?" I asked.

The smile did not leave her face as she answered. "No, he isn't teasing. He just doesn't know a better answer, so I guess that one is as good as any."

By this time we had reached the outskirts of McCamey.

McCamey
1926

MOST BOOMTOWNS GREW FROM SOMETHING—a
crossroads store, a small settlement or a country town. McCamey
grew from absolutely nothing.

A man named George B. McCamey drilled in a gusher way
out in the mesa country between Horsehead Crossing on the Pecos
River and Castle Gap, an early day pass between Castle and King
mountains. The day after the gusher blew in, road graders began
scraping out streets on the greasewood flat. With all that oil, people were sure to come, and a town would be needed. People came
alright, thousands of them. In no time at all McCamey had a
population of fifteen thousand.

Boxcar shacks and cabin tents were built hastily and rented
for twenty-five dollars a month with no utilities of any kind. Two
swiftly erected hotels, the Burleson and the McCamey, were unable to house the mass of people coming into town. Some families
lived in their automobiles or under tarps they strung up without
even a tree to tie them to. Men often paid fifty cents a night to
sleep in the barbers' chairs after they had closed for the day. All
over the area drilling crews were punching holes in search of liquid
gold.

We reached McCamey about eight months after the discovery
well was brought under control. Highway 67, a dirt road coming
into town, became McCamey's main street. Cars and horse-drawn
vehicles churned the unstable soil into loose ruts in dry weather.
When it rained, Main Street became a slushy bog. Trucks and
wagons got stuck whether it was wet or dry. Schoolboys with
donkeys or mules pulling wooden sleds charged a dime to trans-

McCamey the way it looked when I moved there. The Grande Theater billboard on the side of the Hotel McCamey reads, "Esther Ralston in the Spotlight." Abell-Hanger Foundation Collection. Courtesy the Petroleum Museum, Midland, Texas.

port pedestrians across the street, often with disastrous results. In case of a fall in the mud, the ladies grabbed their skirts but the men always grabbed for their hats. The old oil-field adage held true: it almost never rained in West Texas, but once oil was discovered there, the skies opened up with unprecedented regularity.

Main Street was lined with wooden storefronts, each with a porch across its width. The builders did not bother to build them the same height, so negotiating the boardwalk from store to store was an exercise in stepping up and down.

We rented a tent-cabin on the far east end of Main Street. To my great joy the family next door had a brown-haired, brown-eyed girl just my age. Her name was Jewel Oliver, and we soon became inseparable. We slept together on each other's cots, ate

meals with each other's families, and our parents called us the "Gold Dust Twins." Gold Dust was a popular brand of soap powder that featured a picture of twins on its box.

Moving pictures were beginning to be shown in most towns now, and they became our great love. We spent summer afternoons at the Grand Theater on the west end of Main Street, about five or six blocks from our homes. We watched Tom Mix, Fay Wray, Mary Pickford, Constance Bennett and other stars of the black-and-white movies. There was no such thing as an x-rated scene in these first flickering efforts of the film industry, so we were allowed to sit through a feature film, Fox Movietone News and a slapstick comedy twice in one afternoon.

The comedy, a shorter film which always accompanied each

feature film, was like dessert after a meal. I always wanted to see it over and over, especially if it happened to be Charlie Chaplin or Our Gang.

On leaving the theater Jewel and I often had to hurry to reach home before dark. We walked arm-in-arm across the wooden porches, up-and-down, up-and-down, until we reached a certain "rooming house" where three red light bulbs glowed through the night.

Our mothers had warned us, "Stay away from that place," so we always detoured into the middle of the street until we had passed the building. We often discussed what might be taking place there. Finally Jewel asked her mother and reported back to me.

"She said there are women there who sleep with men."

I looked at her quizzically. "Is that all she said?"

"Posa-tive-ly all," Jewel insisted.

"Well," I replied, "my mother sleeps with my father."

"So does mine," she admitted.

We were just as puzzled as ever but a little less fearful of the place. After all, how could sleeping people possibly harm us?

Several days after this we had watched a bone-chilling movie called "The Gorilla" and, of course, we saw it twice. Twilight was deepening when we left the theater. We walked home with our arms linked about each other for courage, our heels clomping like horses' hooves along the boardwalk. But fright was taking us faster and faster. When we reached the red-light rooming house we never faltered but pounded straight across the porch beneath the three red lights and on toward home. Whatever fears that house held for us disappeared completely when compared to the hairy gorilla we could feel breathing down our necks.

A few doors down from the infamous house stood Mc-Camey's self-service grocery, the first such store I had ever seen.

It was called the M System Grocery, for the shelves were arranged in the shape of the letter M. Customers chose their own groceries and placed them on the counter where a clerk added the cost by hand. Heretofore a woman had to ask the clerk for each item. If she wanted a can of corn, that is just what she got because there were no choices of brands, sizes or qualities.

Water was a major problem in those early days in this arid land. Trucks with water tanks drove up and down each street every day selling water. Some of it came in railroad tank cars and some was brought in by tank trucks from Alpine and Fort Stockton where there was an abundance of spring water.

We kept two barrels near our back door. In one we kept water purchased for one dollar a barrel from the truck marked "Alpine Water." This was used only for drinking and cooking, and a tight clean canvas cover was kept over it at all times.

The other barrel was for washing, mopping, bathing and, after boiling, for washing dishes. This water cost fifty cents a barrel and was delivered in a beat-up truck with a makeshift tank on the back and a handmade sign reading "Using Water." It came from the Pecos River or from some rancher's windmill tank and was always muddy.

My mother made good use of every drop of water. Soapy water from the laundry was used to mop the floor and scrub the porches. Rinse water was poured on the small shrubs and vines she insisted on trying to grow. Bath water was also used for floors and for washing the car. When a pail of water had seen every possible use in the household it was poured on a greasewood bush or a small mesquite tree. "Even a tumbleweed needs a drink," Mother said.

In addition to a water supply McCamey needed all other city services. Main Street had all sorts of stores, shops, hotels and banks, but utility companies were yet to come. People interested

111

in making McCamey an enduring city rather than a fly-by-night boomtown were working on its problems, among them our own Mr. Dugan.

Mr. Dugan lived in a little two-room house between and slightly behind two of his business buildings. According to my father his properties had made him a rich man but he was still a kind, wonderful and lonely man. He visited us occasionally, and I always stopped by to see him when I walked down the street. He discussed events of the day with me as if I were an adult.

He was vitally interested in the progress of this town, especially the construction of a jail. He thought it a disgrace that prisoners were chained to posts driven in the ground for want of better facilities. When September came I missed my visits with this dear old friend because school began and we moved off Main Street.

My uncle had purchased one of the new Fordson tractors and contracted to unload the huge timbers, used for building oil derricks, from rail cars. Heretofore all this work had been done using teams of horses or mules, but the machine age was dawning. This labor could be done easier and faster with tractors. My father was working with my uncle, and the two were never happier than when working together. They did well in this work for quite some time, and our meager savings began to grow again.

The Bumgardners had built a small house in McCamey much like the one they had built in the Corsicana field. With fall coming my father wanted us in a house, so he and Uncle Buss bought lumber and built a fifteen-foot shed room on the side of the Bumgardner's house. We each had our own apartment in this forerunner of the duplex.

I loved living with Dellon—he was my live toy. I taught him to ride stick horses, play cowboys and Indians and build roads in the sand for his small cars. He often played dolls with me but was a little rough for paper dolls.

A Fordson tractor equipped with a winch. This was an oil field work-horse used for many tasks. On display at the Petroleum Museum, Midland, Texas. Photo by Dick Stowe.

Each afternoon when I got home from school he was waiting for me, saying "Let's eat on the little table." Our mothers furnished milk or orange juice for the toy teapot and cups and bread-and-butter sandwiches for the little plates. When Aunt Ira wanted to give him Castoria or castor oil she mixed it with the orange juice and he was never the wiser. I was very careful not to drink orange juice that day.

Home life was good but the situation at school needed a lot of improvement. Just as two hotels failed to hold McCamey's overflow of people, so the four-room sheet-iron schoolhouse they had built failed to hold the overflow of oil field kids. Classes were taught in the Methodist Church, which was built like a traditional church with a steeple and bell and wooden pews. This was not the best place to hold classes, but it was better than the hastily

constructed Baptist Church, a gun-barrel tin building with slat benches built for adults. Jewel and I were sent there. Our feet hung several inches off the floor, and our books and pencils kept falling through the slatted seats.

Teachers came and went. A month was the longest one ever stayed, and their teaching methods varied from poor to nonexistent. About the time we learned a teacher's name she disappeared, so we wound up calling each teacher by the name of the one who had preceded her.

One of our teachers, Mrs. Martin, was a strict disciplinarian. For any infraction of her rules she made the offending child stand before an improvised blackboard that stood against the back of a piano, with his nose in a ring. Each arm had to be extended, palm up, and a textbook was placed on each hand. If the crime was great

The entire student body of McCamey's first school, with Mr. W. C. Williamson, the first superintendent of schools, in the fall of 1926.

enough, she drew the nose ring so high the child had to stand on tiptoe to reach it. When the child's arms gave out and the books fell to the floor, the child was told to be seated.

Mrs. Martin was very nervous; any little noise startled her, so books and pencils falling on the floor drove her crazy. Once my friend Jewel had to stand and hold up two history books until her arms ached and she was crying from exhuastion, all because she stubbed her toe on the end of one of the wooden benches as she was marching in. I was so mad at Mrs. Martin I wanted to punch her silly nose.

The very next day my pencil rolled off between the slats and rattled on the floor. I put my nose in the familiar ring and extended my arms as instructed. When Mrs. Martin placed a history book on each hand I pretended that my skinny arms were just too weak to hold them up. She placed them there a second time, and again I let them slide off. She left me standing there a few minutes and sent me to my seat. Kids all over the room were snickering. They knew I had turned cartwheels all my life, and my skinny arms were as strong as my legs. But the teacher didn't know, and nobody told her.

Mrs. Martin left after a few days, and the teacher who followed her played the piano while we marched, sang and played singing games most of every day. Except for what I learned from reading my books when they were first issued to me, a habit I still had, I learned very little that term. But before many months passed, changes were taking place that would mean another move for us.

Structural steel began to replace the wooden timbers traditionally used to build the derricks. Soon no more of the timbers were arriving on the rail cars, and my father and uncle had to find other work for their tractor. It had lost out to heavier machinery. Smaller jobs paid a lot less and were not sufficient to support two families. My father began to talk of having to go back to an oil company, but they tried hard to make their little business hold on.

Finally one Saturday the two men pored over their account books around our table and found that, except for two or three uncollected accounts, they were completely broke. They emptied their wallets on the table. Uncle Buss had a silver dollar and two dimes; my dad had one dollar bill and a little small change.

"I have a dollar," Mother said, "but I need it for a barrel of water this afternoon."

"Hell!" Uncle Buss said. "We haven't got the price of a meal between us."

"Wait," said Aunt Ira. She hurried over to their house and returned with eighteen dollars. "I've saved a little for my trip to Corpus Christi. Maybe that will help."

"We can't take that," Mother objected. "You haven't seen your family in so long . . . "

"Never mind," she said. "It isn't enough for the trip anyway and besides, I like to eat just as well as you do."

They divided the money so that each family would have nine dollars for groceries. It was always that way—what one suffered, we all suffered, and if one had food, we all ate.

The men promised to repay the travel fund as soon as possible. We bought a few groceries for Sunday, and on Monday my father went to the offices of Pure Oil Company to ask for a job.

The only opening was for a pumper switcher on a lease just east of King Mountain.

This time we did not build a tent-cabin or a house. The men removed the shed they had built, moved it to the new location and boarded up the open side. It looked funny with the roof all slanting in one direction, but my father said, "The raindrops will have no trouble deciding which way to run."

My mother drove me to school each morning. I walked to the Bumgardners' after school and waited until Daddy got off work. Both parents came to take me home.

One evening about twilight we had just returned from the Bumgardners' when an automobile came down our dirt road at a fast pace and stopped beside our car. Mother had gone into the house ahead of my father and me, so we turned in time to see a familiar man, carrying a tow-headed boy, rush by us.

"Hello John, hello Estha," he greeted us as he brushed past and entered the house calling, "Mrs. Briscoe, I need your help." It was Clarence Stewart, our neighbor from Santa Rita, with his little Sonny Boy.

The little boy held out his arms as he recognized his favorite sitter. "What's wrong, Clarence?" Mother asked as she took the boy in her arms.

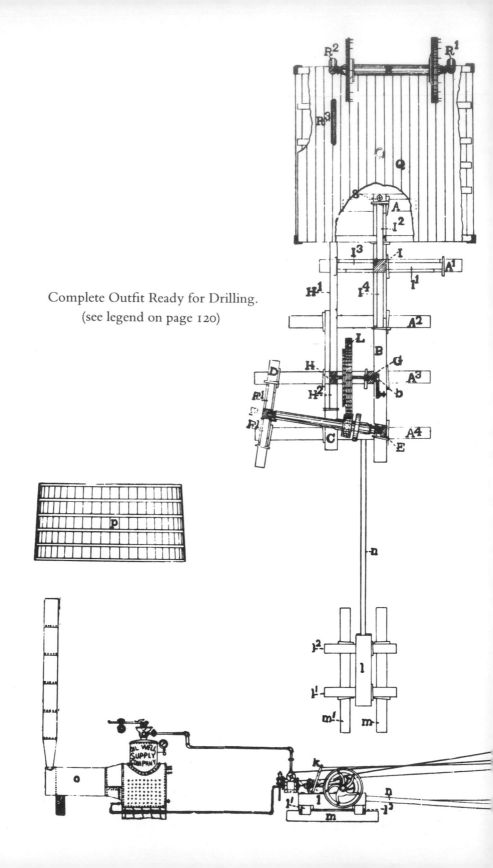

Complete Outfit Ready for Drilling.

(see legend on page 120)

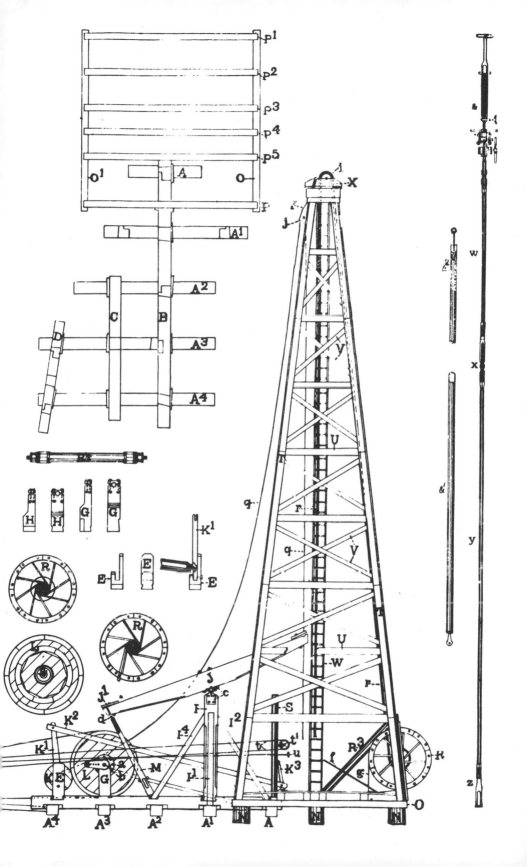

NAMES OF PARTS OF RIG
(reference to pages 118 and 119)

A	Nose Sill or Short Sill under end of Main Sill.
A–1	Mud Sill No. 1.
A–2	" " No. 2.
A–3	" " No. 3.
A–4	" " No. 4.
B	Main "
C	Sub " or Counter Sill.
D	Sand Reel Tail Sill.
E	Knuckle Post.
F	Tail "
F–1	" " Braces.
G	Front Jack Post.
H	Rear Jack Post.
H–1	" " Brace.
H–2	" " "
I	Samson Post.
I–1	" " Brace.
I–2	" " "
I–3	" " "
I–4	" " "
J	Walking Beam.
J–1	" " Cap or Adjuster Board.
K	Sand Reel.
K–1	" " Lever.
K–2	" " Reach.
K–3	" " Handle.
L	Band Wheel.
M	Pitman.
N	Derrick Foundation Posts.
O	" Mud Sill.
O–1	" " "
P	" Floor "
P–1	" " "
P–2	" " "
P–3	" " "
P–4	" " "
P–5	" " "
Q	" " 20 Pieces, 2 × 12 inches × 20 ft.
R	Bull Wheels.
R–1	" " Post.
R–2	Bull Wheel Post.
R–3	" " " Brace.
S	Head Ache Post.
T	Derrick Corner.
U	" Girt.
V	" Brace.
W	" Ladder.
X	Crown Block.
Y	Sand Pump Pulley Block.
a	Flanges.
b	Shaft Crank and Wrist Pin.
c	Saddle and Side Irons.
d	Stirrup.
e	Drilling Hook.
f	Brake Lever.
g	" Band.
h	" Staple.
i	Crown Pulley.
j	Sand Pump Pulley.
k	Engine.
l	" Block.
l–1	" Pony Sill.
l–2	" " "
m	" Mud "
m–1	" " "
n	" Block, Brace (or Bumper)
o	Boiler
p	Tank.
q	Sand Line.
r	Cable.
s	Bull Rope.
t	Telegraph Cord.
t–1	" Wheel.
u	Reverse Cord.
v	Rope Socket.
w	Sinker Bar.
x	Jars.
y	Auger Stem.
z	Drilling Bit.
&	Temper Screw.
&–1	Bailer.
&–2	Sand Pump.

"Esther is in the hospital with our new baby, and she's not doing well at all. Could you keep Sonny for a few days?"

Of course, the answer was yes.

Clarence left us with a paper bag full of clothing he had hastily gathered. We found three little socks, no two of which were mates, several pairs of overalls, one shirt and only one pair of training pants. There were no sleepers and no sweater or jacket. Mother pulled out her remnant bag and began sewing.

The tot seemed content with us as long as my father did not hug or kiss my mother. My father laughingly threatened him, "I'm gonna send you home, young man, so I can kiss my wife."

I couldn't wait to get home from school each evening to play with Sonny before his bedtime. My dad made him a stick horse and a little wooden car with soda pop bottle caps for wheels. Mother taught him to eat with a fork. Ten days later, when his father came for him, she had finished three small shirts, five training pants, and a little coat made from the good parts of one of her old skirts. She had also made a dress for the new baby.

We were happy to hear that Esther was at home and both she and the baby doing well, but for many days after Sonny Boy left us it was lonely at the foot of King Mountain.

I enjoyed the mountain. Several girlfriends spent weekends with me, and we explored the mountain as far as we could climb. This was the beginning of my lifelong love for mountains.

During the blustery days of March the company transferred my father to yet another boomtown called Crane. By this time I should have become accustomed to saying goodbye to my dear friends, but it was no easier to leave Jewel than it had been to leave any of the others. In fact, moving became a little harder each time, and I felt that life just held too many partings. But we sold our one-sided house and moved to Crane.

A spudder showing drill bit, bailer, and wooden tank. On display at the Petroleum Museum, Midland, Texas. Photo by Dick Stowe.

Crane
1927

CRANE WAS A DUSTY, WIND-BLOWN BOOMTOWN with the customary wooden storefronts and boardwalks, situated at the north end of Castle Mountain near the historic Castle Gap and just north of Horsehead Crossing on the Pecos River. The gap and crossing were well-known to Indians and early settlers since both the Butterfield and the Overland stagecoach lines crossed the Pecos here, along with the Goodnight-Loving cattle trail.

Crane County covered 796 square miles, and Crane was its only town and post office. Not that more of either were needed, for virtually the entire population, before the arrival of oil drillers, was contained on one or two large ranches.

Streets had been bladed off for the city but with the March winds blasting the loose sand about with such abandon we could never have found the streets except for the rows of tent-cabins with open areas between.

We set up a tent-cabin like all the rest so that we could live in town and I could go to school while Daddy drove to the lease every day to work. No public schools had been established, so I was enrolled in a small subscription school within walking distance of our home.

The teacher's husband had built the neat but small one-room school building. It was outfitted with chairs and tables for all sizes of children, and we had brightly painted cabinets and lockers for our belongings. The walls were painted in cheerful colors, and our teacher was a delightful young woman. She taught children in all seven grades, but since the tuition was considered very high at five dollars a month, she only had about twenty children. In addition to the three Rs, she taught us songs from records she played on her Victrola. We were issued brand new textbooks from the best publishers.

I read those new books as fast as I could. I still loved books and could never get my hands on enough to read. Also, I was conscious of the constant threat of having to move away before the books were completed, so I made sure not to miss the last part. There was one book, however, that I did not read; in fact, I opened it as little as possible. That was my arithmetic book.

Our frequent moves kept me mathematically confused. I repeated some lessons and completely missed others, leaving gaps in my mathematical education that made it harder for me as I went along. I chose to ignore the problem, hoping it would go away, while it slowly became a monster that would almost devour me.

The weather in Crane during March and April could be described with one word—sandstorm. Our scanty furniture stayed covered with the gritty stuff. We had to shake our sheets before going to bed at night and wash each dish, pot or pan before using it.

One afternoon I struggled home from school against the strong blasts of wind-blown sand to find Mother under the bedcovers, head and all. The white bedspread covering her was golden with drifted sand. As I proceeded to make my favorite snack, crackers with mustard and peanut butter, the oilcloth was just as golden. I cleaned a spot with a dish towel and smeared the goodies on my crackers. Mother poked her head out, turtle-fashion, and asked, "How do you know you're not eating sand?"

"It doesn't grit," I answered.

"Then eat it quick before it does," she replied.

Mother never complained about the sandstorms or our frugal way of life. She loved West Texas and credited it with saving her life. My father liked the West too but he often remarked, "Someday we're going to live better than this." I had no memory of anything but oil field life, so it seemed normal to me.

The month of May came in like a sparking jewel after the two preceding months. The sandstorms had blown themselves out, and it was warm enough to play outdoors. Our teacher furnished us new baseballs, bats and volleyballs. It was a great time to be alive.

Then one Monday morning I went to school and found the door locked. All the children played around waiting for the teacher, but she never came. Finally we knocked on the door of her residence which stood just behind the school building. A man opened the door just a crack and growled at us, "You kids go on home. There ain't gonna be no school today." Later a hand-lettered sign appeared on the schoolhouse door: "No School."

A week later the sign was still on the door. My mother decided an explanation was past due, so she rapped on the man's door and demanded to know what was happening. He told her a tearful story. His wife had run away with a tool-dresser who worked the shift opposite him on a drilling rig. My soft-hearted mother was so sorry for the man that she offered to help him return the children's belongings, check their books in and close the school. Since the teacher had apparently disposed of our report cards from other schools, we were left with no record of the work we had done that year, before or after we came to Crane.

With no more school for the year, we decided to move our tent-cabin out nearer my father's job. He chose a little hill near a windmill and set our tent slightly above the settlement that had grown up along a row of small mesquite bushes. "The weather will soon be hot, and we'll be cooler up here where the breeze can catch us," he explained.

A dozen or more families had, through force of habit, settled near the windmill even though the water, loaded with gyp-

Crane, Texas, 1927. When we arrived in Crane, hundreds of tents and derricks covered the landscape. Abell-Hanger Foundation Collection. Courtesy the Petroleum Museum, Midland, Texas.

sum, was unusable. It was called gyp water and even the cattle would not drink it. All our water had to be hauled from a lease near town.

About a mile west of us stood a large teaming camp where huge, circus-type tents had been set up to house and feed the mule skinners, the men who drove the multiple teams of mules and operated the large machinery and wagons they powered.

We set up our usual twelve-by-fourteen tent-cabin with the table and chairs in the middle of the room. Three new pieces of furniture had been added: Mother had a new Singer Sewing Machine, treadle model, we had a small wooden three-door refrigerator to keep blocks of ice we brought from town, and we had a new, late-model Florence Kerosene Range for cooking.

The gleaming white range was Mother's joy. It stood on four

tall legs which supported the row of four wick-type burners. A shiny oven covered two of the burners. The white enamel back board extended behind the burners to a top shelf which reached the length of the stove. A glass reservoir on one end of the stove kept "glug-glugging" as the kerosene was fed into the burners. A heat indicator on the front of the oven assured approximately the desired temperature. It was quite the fanciest stove we had ever seen, and when Mother began turning out pies, cakes and breads we all agreed that the stove was worth every penny it cost, though it was thirty-two dollars and fifty cents, "quite a lot for a poor man to pay," according to my father.

General Stonewall Jackson also brought new joy to our family. Stony, as we called him, was a German Shepherd puppy who belonged to a truck driver we called Shorty. Shorty had bought

127

Stony to keep him company in the truck, but the dog was suffering from the engine heat inside the truck. We agreed to keep him until he grew tall enough to sit up and look out the window. I kept telling myself not to love him too much because I could not keep him long. But his stay with us was pure joy.

Stony and I played with all the kids in the settlement. He played fielder on our baseball team and even tried to jump rope with the girls. He helped himself to a cool drink from the drip pan under the refrigerator and helped me gather sticks for Mother to burn under her washpot. The gyp water tank became his private bathtub, and he jumped in several times a day only to jump out again and shake water all over everyone unlucky enough to be near. I was sure I could see a smile on his face when we all scattered to avoid a soaking.

Late one afternoon Stony and I were playing hopscotch with the kids beside our tent. There had been a few clouds with a little lightning and thunder over Castle Mountain that morning, but the sun was shining brightly on the desert, and the cool breeze from the mountain showers was welcome.

Suddenly we heard shouting and looked down the hill toward the row of tents. An old man with a long white beard and long flowing white hair was running along hitting each tent with a stick he carried. "RUN!" he shouted. "It's a flood, a flood!" He kept shouting "Flood! Flood!" as he ran on down the line of the old fence toward the teaming camp in the distance. We never saw him again.

Our mothers all gathered, laughing and saying such things as "Who was that? Noah?" and "What's wrong with him?" or "A flood on his desert?" We had stopped our games and joined the laughter when we heard a loud noise none of us could identify. Looking toward the mountain we saw, coming across the flat arid plain, a wall of water about six feet high and wide enough to wipe out a small city.

Screaming women and children scrambled up the hill toward

us. They all stood beside our tent and watched as water from a cloudburst on the mountain wiped out every tent along the mesquite-lined arroyo. The water lapped a scant eight feet from the top of the knoll where my father had so fortunately located our home.

Ours was the only home left standing as the dirty water swirled on to the teaming camp and completely destroyed the mess tent where the cooks had long tables of hot supper waiting for about a hundred hungry men.

The flood continued a ways along the flat desert floor until it was finally swallowed by the hot sand. By noon of the next day the sand along its path of destruction was hot and dry again as if the flood had never happened.

My mother and father had stayed up all night the first night making pallets for the children all over our floor. For several days we walked up and down the fence row, helping the neighbors salvage what belongings they could. One little girl found her favorite dress hanging from the top of a mesquite tree, but we were only able to find one of her patent leather slippers mired in the caked sand.

Nobody in 1927 had heard of disaster relief. These people had to pick themselves up and start over. In most cases the man of the family had driven to work in the car, so it was saved and that was a start. For several days and nights my parents kept dipping into their savings to help feed and house these people. They loaned several of them money to buy a tent and bedding, never expecting them to be able to repay it. Payment for their generosity seemed to come from the fact that they were able to give help instead of needing it themselves.

Many people remarked that we were lucky because our belongings were spared but luck, I think, was only a part of it. My father said, "I was afraid there must be some reason those mesquites were taller along that old fence row."

Most of the families hit by the flood left the windmill area, leaving me without playmates, so Stony and I played alone. We were all lonely without neighbors and glad to learn that a traveling carnival had set up in Crane.

Carnivals drew capacity crowds in oil field towns because there were so few opportunities for family entertainment or recreation. My father and I loved carnivals and the ferris wheel was our favorite ride, but Mother refused to ride with us. Once, near McCamey, Daddy and I got stuck on top of the wheel when the engine pulling the ride broke down. After waiting over an hour while the young ride operator tried to start the engine, Mother got in the car, drove to the Bumgardners' house and brought Uncle Buss back with a small toolbox in his hand. He had the engine running in a short time, but Mother declared, "You're never getting on another one of those things." She relented, though, when we went to the carnival in Crane one night right after supper. Daddy and I rode the ferris wheel while Mother, as usual, kept both feet on the ground.

She did agree to ride the hobby horses with me, for that was a much gentler ride. The wooden horses were anchored to a revolving platform and moved up and down to the music of the carousel.

Since I had always wanted a Kewpie doll with a feather dress, we set out to try to win one. Mother thought she could win one by pitching darts to break balloons. She was surprisingly good at it but not quite good enough for a Kewpie, though she did win a carnival glass bowl.

Next I tried my luck at fishing with a small tea strainer, but the wooden fishes I caught were the wrong numbers to win a prize. Daddy chose baseballs at a quarter for four. He kept buying balls and chunking away until he finally hit a bullseye. It must have cost him twice what the chalk doll was worth, but I happily chose the Kewpie with red feathers.

When we got home I found that the Kewpie looked just great standing on Mother's sewing machine, so I left it there. Daddy rolled up the tent flaps to catch the breeze through the screens, and we went to bed.

During the night the desert breeze grew stronger, and a loud crash startled us awake. Stony emerged from his favorite bed beneath the table, barking as if to roust an army. Daddy lit the kerosene lamp, and there was my beautiful Kewpie reduced to hunks of chalk all over the floor.

We all tried to go back to sleep but Stony did not understand that the danger was past. He stood guard the rest of the night beside my bed, and every time I stirred he jumped to protect me, all twenty toenails rattling against the linoleum. Next morning Mother patted his head as she sympathized, "I don't blame you, boy. That darned Kewpie made a nervous wreck out of me too."

I did not weep for the lost Kewpie. I figured the dolls were like balloons, never meant to last long. I fitted the red feather around Mother's hand mirror and kept the chunks of chalk in a box. They would be great for drawing hopscotch marks on sidewalks, next time we had a sidewalk.

Not long after the desert flood we were offered a company house on a lease, not far from the company toolhouse. Stony had grown quite tall, and it was time for him to go back to Shorty. I had known all along that he was not my dog, but giving him up was very hard. The blow was softened somewhat by the fact that Shorty worked out of the nearby toolhouse and I could see Stony every morning and evening.

Stony was always happy to see me and licked my face clean every time, but he seemed to understand that it was his job to ride in the swamper's seat and guard the truck.

One afternoon as Shorty was checking tools in at the toolhouse, Stony found a cool shady spot and stretched out for a nap.

Unfortunately the spot was just behind the back wheel of another truck. The trucker did not notice the dog and backed the truck over his head and neck, crushing him into the deep sand.

Mother and I heard the men shouting and ran to the toolhouse. The men were discussing what to do. The nearest veterinarian was probably a hundred miles away, so they decided the humane thing to do was to shoot the dog to relieve his misery. I could see tears in Shorty's eyes, and I begged and cried until Shorty relented and said, "We'll wait a few hours and see what happens."

Since the toolshed was elevated on posts to make its dock even with the truck beds, we made a bed for Stony under the shed on the soft sand. Shorty and I took turns caring for him, dissolving aspirin tablets in water and dripping the medicine down his crushed throat. I spent each day with him, and Shorty spread a bedroll beside him and spent his nights there. Mother boiled beef bones and made a broth for us to feed him, one drop at a time. He slept a lot and held on to life.

Ten days later he showed improvement. Finally he was well enough to be carried to our house, where we fed him all he could eat until his gaunt look was gone and he became playful again. Everyone agreed that the soft sand saved his life.

Too soon the day came when I had to give him back to Shorty because Shorty was moving to another lease. Stony seemed to know what was expected of him that morning when Mother, Daddy and I stood in front of the little house while Shorty parked the truck, opened the door and whistled for him. Stony licked us goodbye and trotted to the truck, then turned and trotted back to lick off the tears that streamed down my face.

Then he climbed into the swamper's seat and sat, tall and dignified, his beautiful coat and perfect profile revealing his noble ancestry. Eyes forward, as if into battle, he rode away. That was the last time I saw General Stonewall Jackson. We had a note from

Shorty later, telling us that Stony was fully recovered but every time he saw a dark-haired girl about my size, he checked her out very carefully.

Our home was lonely without Stony. I had only two or three playmates, children who had moved to the lease from the desert flood area. Most of these families were doing well now, and every payday my father brought home money that one of them had repaid. Usually the money was accompanied by a note of thanks and gratitude.

Throughout our oil field days this is the sort of honest, hard-working, family-oriented people we came to know. Of course there were gamblers, con artists, alcoholics, thieves, prostitutes and every other form of undesirable character present in the boomtowns, but it was ordinary, salt-of-the-earth citizens who built the towns, schools and churches and established the oil industry. They were pioneers in the same sense that settlers in wagon trains were pioneers, and they suffered the same exposure to the elements.

The men who worked outdoors in August's desert heat earned every penny of the five dollars they were paid each day. My father was becoming exhausted by the heat and hard work. He found himself near the house one August noonday and stopped in to eat lunch with Mother and me. After lunch he stretched out on the floor in front of the door with a chair cusion under his head. His eyes were closed, and we tiptoed, letting him nap briefly before returning to the visible heat waves that shimmered above the burning sands outside. However, he was not asleep.

He sat up abruptly and said, "Viney, let's throw some clothes in the car and go to Brady and Pecan Gap."

"When?"

"Tomorrow. I want to see as many of our kinfolk as I can in two weeks."

"But, can you get off work?"

"I'll just take off without pay. I'll tell them today—and I'll ask to be sent back to McCamey before school starts."

"Hooray! I'll be in McCamey in time for school!" I wanted to explore that thought further but there was no time because Mother was already tossing out clothes to be laundered before we packed them. We both knew that when my Dad decided to do something, immediate action was far too slow for him.

Next morning, before the sun rose, we had loaded boxes, bags and suitcases in the car, locked the house and were on our way east.

Back to Our Beginnings

WE SPENT THE FIRST NIGHT of our trip at a tourist court somewhere in the Barnhart-San Angelo area. The cabin held nothing but a bed, a dresser and a hot plate but the owner brought in a cot for me. A community bathroom in the center of the court served all the rooms. We thought these accommodations quite nice for three dollars. Mother cooked breakfast with a coffeepot and skillet she had brought along in our old chuckbox. The box also held crackers, cheese, sardines and the pork and beans that my father detested for lunch.

Very late in the afternoon we crossed Brady Creek at the same fateful crossing, but we used the bridge this time. We drove into Aunt Lillie's backyard honking like mad. We hadn't told them we were coming because there was no time and besides, we wanted to surprise them.

It was fun to see Aunt Lillie come out on the front porch wiping her hands on her apron and calling, "Henry, look who's here!" She cooked fried chicken and hot biscuits with gravy for supper, and my cousins babied me as usual. Belvery took me for a horseback ride, and Abbie sat on the floor and made paper doll furniture for me.

The next day we went to see Granny Pearl, Grandfather Bumgardner, Homer and Charlie. Then we spent two days making calls on cousins, aunts and uncles in Brady. Mother's cousin Bedie had married Leo Moore, a butcher shop owner. Their son, Leicester, who was about my age, took me to the shop, for I had never seen a butcher shop before. Mr. Moore, a short, stocky man with highly developed biceps and a large handlebar mustache, was completely enveloped in a starched white apron. He had just placed what appeared to be half of some sort of animal on the chopping block. One leg stuck out at a grotesque angle, and the whole thing was bloody. I felt a little sick, but curiosity kept me watching as he wielded the huge cleaver with a practiced swing. Chop! Chop! With ease the huge beef was cut into pieces. Then he wiped his bloody hands on his now blood-streaked apron and began wrapping the pieces in white paper from a large roll on the counter. He handed me one of the large white packages.

"Take this to Mrs. Bumgardner and tell her to cook it for your supper," he said.

Next morning Mother said, "Today we are going to see the uncle who gave you your name." This was my father's brother, Elbert, next in age to my father. He and my father could have been mistaken for twins; both were small men with the same facial features, dark hair and hazel eyes. They even moved with the same vigorous gait. I was born just before Uncle Elbert went off to France during World War I, and he named me Estha for the fiance who would wait for his return. Not long after he left, the influenza epidemic took her life. A few years after he returned to farm in McCulloch County, he married Lois Bratten, a charming lady who taught primary grades in the local school.

I loved my Aunt Lois so much that I secretly wished I had been named for her. In her patient and concise way she answered my incessant questions about teaching school and was concerned about the education I was getting in oil field schools. Later I heard her diplomatically mentioning to my father that she hoped we would be able to live near a good school through my high school years. He assured her that he was working toward that goal.

The next afternoon my mother was ready to go again. "This time," she said, "I'll take you to meet the doctor who brought you into the world."

Gray-haired, kindly Doctor Powell was a typical old-time

family doctor who delivered babies, set broken bones and made house calls, using a horse and buggy until recently. His office was an interesting clutter of papers, books, medical supplies and instruments. He seated us beside his desk and turned in a high-backed swivel chair to face us. He wore a white shirt with a tie, a dark suit with a vest and a gold watch chain across his portly midsection from pocket to pocket.

We had much to talk about, for he was the grandfather of my cousin, Mary Ruth, a vivacious blonde near my own age whom I had not seen in a very long time. Mother and I wanted to hear all about Ruth and her mother, where they lived and what their life was like.

Doctor Powell's daughter, Mary, was my mother's good friend. She had married my father's oldest brother, Arthur. The couple were divorced when Ruth was five years old and since Ruth moved from place to place with her mother I did not get to see her often. Our enjoyable chat with the doctor was cut short when patients began arriving.

Next morning we had to move on to Pecan Gap, so we stopped at Grandfather Bumgardner's grocery store as we were leaving town. The large sacks of flour and meal with my grandfather's picture on them still stood all around the counters. My grandfather, as always, beckoned me behind the curved glass candy counter where he filled a bag with candy and gave it to me to take on the trip. I thanked him, then hesitated, wanting to give him a kiss but not knowing how. He stood so tall! If he smiled, it was a small smile, undetectable beneath his mustache and beard. I thanked him again and went away, clutching the paper bag and reasoning to myself, "I know he loves me because he always gives me candy." My quandary came, I believe, because of the vast difference in personality between my two grandfathers.

When we reached Grandfather Briscoe's house late in the afternoon, the scene was different. He met us at the car, a tall, angular man with laughing gray eyes and a mustache. Grabbing me in a bear hug, he kissed me until I squealed, "Your mustache tickles!" Then he gave my mother the same treatment.

Next came Grandmother, a short, plump figure with her gray hair pinned back tight. She was wearing her customary cotton housedress with long sleeves. "Well, I'll say!" she exclaimed. "Just look how my little Estha has grown." I was born in this grandmother's home when she lived in Waldrip, and she reportedly told my father, "This child can play with anything in my house except the hammer and the mirror."

Then I was enfolded in a pair of long bony arms belonging to my lanky eighteen-year-old uncle, Hobert, youngest of Grandmother's nine children. He kissed me and passed on to my parents. The Briscoe family loved everybody and always kissed friends and relatives.

My grandfather, along with three of his brothers, had come to Texas from Alabama about 1890. Grandmother, who by then had three children, followed him by train. The couple never returned to Alabama, even for a visit, because they never felt able to leave the responsibilities of family and farm.

My father's brother, Edwin, always known as Poke, remained in the family home and joined his father in farming. He and his wife, Vay, who grew up on a neighborhing farm, now had two children, Edwin, Jr., and Charline. Edwin, Jr., was only about six years old but already showed promise of attaining the more-than-six-foot height of his mother's brothers. Charline, three, was a tiny bit of a girl with hair the color of the cotton that burst from the ripe bolls all around their farmhouse in the black earth of Delta County. Poke had an exceptional tenor voice and was in demand as a soloist for weddings and funerals. Aunt Vay also enjoyed singing, and the couple took part in the Sunday afternoon singing conventions made popular in East Texas by such religious singing groups as the Stamps Quartet.

The farmhouse had huge rooms, bigger than most school-rooms in the oil fields. The floors were wood, scrubbed white with lye soap. Wide porches almost circled the house, and tall bushy chinaberry trees shaded it from the August sun. A well with a rope and bucket stood not far from the back step. The yard around the house had been swept until it was hard and smooth. A storm cellar in the side yard held vegetables from the garden, canned in glass jars, as well as boxes of onions, potatoes, pears, pumpkins and watermelons to be carried into winter. A wooden smokehouse in the backyard held pork and hams that had been raised and cured on the farm. Beyond the yard were barns and fenced lots for the cows and horses. Farm machinery—plows, harrows and scrapers—stood near the barns.

Grandmother's furniture was simple. Except for the chiffo-robe in her guest room and the large marble-topped dresser in her own bedroom, most of it was handmade. The kitchen table, long enough to serve nine children, and its long benches were crafted by my grandfather's hands. Cane-bottom chairs were used throughout the house, and there was always a wooden rocking chair beside the churn where Grandmother made butter.

The sheets and pillowcases that Aunt Vay and Grandmother kept on the beds were starched and ironed, and many of them were decorated with embroidery, crochet or tatting. Aunt Vay was a creative needlewoman.

A large table, larger than the kitchen table, stood on the back porch. A huge galvanized pan, about four inches deep, held water for cooling the giant earthenware crocks of milk. A white cloth, something like a sheet, was dipped into the water and drawn up over the crocks. It had to be dipped several times a day to keep the fresh milk as cool as possible. Half a dozen shiny milk pails hung on nails around the top of the screened porch.

When my father, who had grown up in a home just like this, came for a visit it was like the return of the prodigal. A celebration was in order. All nearby relatives and friends began arriving, and the relatives stayed overnight. First came my grandfather's youngest brother, Walter, and his family from a farm a few miles away. My great-uncle Walter was a short, balding man with a cheerful face. He and his wife, Essie, a lissome woman wearing a bright print dress with a matching sunbonnet, rode high on the spring seat of their farm wagon. Their car was too small to accommodate the family along with all the extra bedding, chairs and food they were bringing to help with the entertainment. Four children rode on chairs in the wagon. Their oldest son, Weldon, and their daughter, Laverne, were grownups to me, in their late teens like my uncle Hobert. Wayne and Jack were near my age, and I enjoyed playing with them. Wayne was a quiet, introspective boy but Jack was a chatterbox like me.

Next came the Wrights, Aunt Verna and Uncle Burney. I had not seen them since we left Mexia to go west. They were both studying at East Texas State Teachers College and would soon be teachers.

The women helped Aunt Vay and Grandmother as they cooked in pans that seemed large enough for an army kitchen. These women were accustomed to cooking for large families and often several farmhands as well. The tiny cooking utensils in my mother's kitchen seemed toylike by comparison.

About twenty people ate at Grandmother's table that night, and all the women and girls helped with the dishes while Aunt Vay and Grandmother made pallets on the floor, using bright-colored patchwork quilts topped with clean white sheets. The kids would be needing them later.

After supper the adults gathered chairs out under the chinaberry trees, laughing and talking, learning who got married, had a baby or died since they last got together. The cousins played together all around the house and yard. First we caught lightning bugs and put them in jars; then we played hide-and-seek in the moonlight. But when the adults began to sing, all play stopped and we gathered around to join in. I thought this was the most beautiful singing I had ever heard. My grandparents and their children had been singing together around an old pump organ in their fireplace room since all the children were small. They began with such songs as "Shall We Gather at the River" or "When the Roll is Called up Yonder." Then they sang "K-K-Katy," "Seeing Nellie Home," and "The Whippoorwill Song." Grandmother, in her high sweet voice, always sang the part of the whippoorwill. It made goose bumps on my arms.

An eleven-year-old's legs are a bit long for sitting on laps, but I took turns with Aunt Verna and Uncle Burney. I wanted to hear all about the college courses they were taking, and after talking with them I felt that I really must go to college and become a teacher—that is, if I didn't decide to become a movie star. It was going to be a hard choice.

Too soon we had to turn the little blue Overland west again, and we drove straight through the middle of downtown Dallas. We planned to stop and have lunch with my youngest aunt, Madge, who two years earlier had married a Delta County boy named Lee Quate. Lee went to work for a lumber company, and they moved to the Big City.

Mother wanted to take the recommended route to the Quate apartment, but Daddy and I wanted to see the big buildings. We had heard that one of them was twenty-eight stories tall.

"We'll get lost and never find the house," Mother predicted.

"If we do, we'll stop and ask someone how to get there," he assured her as he drove toward downtown Dallas.

We seemed to be driving through a tunnel, the buildings were so tall on each side of the street. I wanted to stop and ride on the trolley cars that ran between the tall buildings and on down the street, but Daddy said there was no place to stop. We saw the twenty-eight-story Magnolia Building towering above the others, and Daddy said someone had told him that a huge sign, at least two stories tall, was being built for the top of the building. We could see no evidence of the project, and it was a least a year later that the flying red horse became a Dallas landmark.

Daddy guessed which turn to take to reach Aunt Madge's house, and he was lucky. We drove straight to the Maple Avenue address. Madge was ten years old when I was born at Grandmother's house and, I was told, played with me like a rag doll. As I grew up, she gave me her undivided attention each time I visited my grandparents until she became a young woman with more adult interests.

Madge prepared lunch, and Uncle Lee dropped by to eat with us, driving a truck with the name of a lumber company painted on the door. Uncle Lee was a tall, erect young man with smooth dark hair and handsome features. Even in his work clothes he looked well dressed. I thought he was the handsomest man I had ever seen. When he smiled his special smile at me and said, "Hello there, Kiddo," I forgave him for all the times my aunt had stopped playing with me, gone in the parlor and closed the door just because her beau had come to call.

After lunch we left the big city and drove out winding Proctor Road through the Trinity River farm area to the Union Bower community, where yet another of my father's brothers lived. This uncle was named Ollie Albert, but some joker in his childhood nicknamed him Polly and it stuck. His wife's name was Charlie, and I was confused. Was it Aunt Charlie and Uncle Polly or the other way around? I remedied this by calling him Uncle Ollie—after all, that's what Grandmother named him.

Uncle Ollie was another small man like my father. He worked for Butler Brothers, a wholesale firm in Dallas. He and Aunt Charlie preferred living in the country so they could have a garden and chickens. Aunt Charlie loved to have someone brush her long dark hair, so she sat on a stool and I played beauty operator while she and Mother admired the lovely embroidered baby clothes she had made for the child she was expecting in a few months. She had lined a baby basket in a pink silky material, and I remembered it when we received a card announcing the arrival of Charles Albert.

We spent the night in Union Bower and were off the next morning to another big city—Fort Worth—to visit the Baker family. Baby Juanita, Aunt Lela's first blonde child, had joined Vivian, Bill and Louise since we last saw them; the baby was seven months old now. This was the first time I noticed that Aunt Lela's mannerisms were so much like those of my mother. The look in those dark Bumgardner eyes was the same too. That was before I realized I had those eyes myself.

That night I enjoyed playing with my three cousins and loving the new baby cousin. Aunt Lela's babies were so pretty that I wished she would have a dozen. She said, "Maybe I'll do that, just for you." She didn't though; she stopped at eight.

After we left Fort Worth we made no more visits, not because there were no more relatives on the way but because our time was running out. The long road back to the oil patch seemed much shorter with all our experiences to discuss on the way.

Daddy had managed to see an unbelievable number of relatives in two weeks. We had seen every aunt and uncle on both sides of my family except my father's oldest sister, Loice Looney, who lived in Weslaco, Texas, with her husband and two daughters. My parents seemed happy and ready to return to work. With so much family love to base their lives on, they seemed to feel secure even though the term "itinerant oil fielders" definitely applied to us.

Mother had to rest in bed for several days after we returned to Crane. She had neglected her rest periods while we traveled but seemed to suffer no ill effects from the trip. Daddy went to work immediately but was told he could make plans to return to Mc-Camey before September 15 when school would start. We heard that McCamey had been busy enlarging its school building so that it held all the classes now. I looked forward to the beginning of school and wondered if any of my friends still lived in McCamey.

For many nights I lay on my cot before going to sleep, recounting the people and events of our trip. It was pleasant to drift off to sleep remembering the high sweet voice of my grandmother singing, "Whippoor—will, Whippoor—will."

McCamey Again
1927

THE NEWS WAS OUT! My sixth grade class was to have a man teacher! As we met in little groups on the schoolground, we could talk of nothing else. Would he be strict? Would we like him? I was happy to discover several of my former classmates still in Mc-Camey, including Jewel Oliver. We resumed our friendship where it had left off.

My father built us a small house on the lot next to the Bumgardners', which was now on the northeast edge of the McCamey airport. The house was made of new lumber with a tar-paper roof. Each tack that held the tar paper in place was driven through a shiny round disk to keep it from cutting through the paper and causing a leak. We never bothered to paint these houses, for we never lived in one long enough for the boards to become weathered. I was very proud of this house. Every afternoon as I walked home from school I could see the metal disks shining in the sunlight. Nobody else had such a shiny roof. We were told that pilots coming into the airport were often guided by the shiny housetop.

The house was twenty by twenty feet square, and the floor was covered with linoleum. The furniture was arranged just as our tent-cabins had been except the table was moved to one side to accommodate a round black sheet-iron heater with a stovepipe that extended through the roof. Throughout the winter we burned chunks of coke in the heater, and it kept the cabin toasty warm.

In May of that year a young aviator named Charles Lindbergh had flown his airship, "Spirit of St. Louis," non-stop from New York to Paris, France, in just thirty-three and one-half hours. It seemed that Mr. Thomas back in Forest Glade School had been right—airplanes were becoming popular.

Dellon and I liked to watch the planes as they landed and took off just beyond our backyards. Dellon probably dreamed of the day he would fly one, but I didn't imagine that they would ever replace our Overland for traveling.

A small plane crashed one day very near the Bumgardners' backyard. I was in school, but Dellon witnessed it all and promptly began building small wooden airplanes and crashing them into the ground. I regretted missing the excitement, but Aunt Ira said, "It was terrible. You were better off in school."

Mr. Hallmark, our teacher, was a handsome young man not long out of college. The girls fell in love with him at first sight, and when the boys on the playground called him "Ole Man Hallmark" we chased them and threatened to tell on them.

Mr. Hallmark had a rule about lessons. If we came to class without reading our history, geography or reading lesson, he gave us five swats on our open palm with a wooden ruler. My friend Christine reported that this hurt terribly, but my habit of reading through each book as soon as it was issued to me saved me from this experience.

Near the middle of October the Oliver family moved back to their former home in San Saba, Texas, and I was lonely again. I had a lot of girlfriends now, but none of them could replace "my" Jewel. It seemed that I must always have one friend that was closer and more special to me than all the rest.

About this time I began keeping lists of my friends in a small red notebook someone had given me. The first entry on November 17, 1927, reads: "My friends are Fay Bowman, Jewel Battles, Helen Bell, Pauline Sherman, Christine Brannan, and Clairene Stephens."

The next diary entry on was on December 9, almost a month later. It reads: "I was moved from Mr. Hallmark's home room to

Grade 6 at the McCamey school, 1927. Teacher T. C. Hallmark is on the left, with Superintendent W. C. Williamson on the right.

Miss Mistrot's room, and my favorite friends are Juanita Bolton, Jewel Battles, Geneva Barnett and Erma Bell Davis."

Friends were very important to me, and I tried to make as many as possible, but they were all girls. I thought boys were far too silly and only wanted to grab our books or pencils or the barrettes from our hair in order to make us chase them. But I did enjoy chasing them.

Miss Adele Mistrot was a doll. Nothing ever disturbed her winning smile or her good humor. Even Allen, our class cut-up, became a different boy after she convinced him that he was a "real gentleman." At Christmas time she must have spent a month's salary on gifts for us. Each girl received a boxed pink powder puff with a small china doll forming a handle on top of the puff. The boys' gift was a small silver pocketknife with a special blade for cleaning fingernails, a heretofore alien task to most of them.

To show our love for this lady we decided to give her a fruit shower. A committee was formed to make the plans. The event was to take place immediately following afternoon recess on a Friday. The committee slipped into the room during recess and decorated the desk with crepe paper and piled it high with fruit and goodies that the children had brought. We held small wrapped candies and gum in our hands and, as usual, Miss Mistrot walked behind us as we filed into the room and stood beside our desks. When she reached her desk a look of surprise lit her face, and she forgot to say "Be seated." Then we all shouted "Shower!" and threw the candies and gum toward the ceiling, letting them rain down about her and her desk.

Mr. Williams, our principal, had kept Miss Mistrot busy on the schoolground to give us time to prepare the surprise. When he opened the door and peeked in, he was invited to join us as we passed goodies to everyone. He complimented us on the way we had planned and presented the shower, making us feel very grown-up. Miss Mistrot dispensed with lessons for the remainder of the afternoon and read to us, for the fourth time, the story of Black Beauty.

It was a good Christmas that year with the Bumgardners right next door. Dellon began looking for Santa Claus before Thanksgiving. His favorite gift was a toy Fordson tractor made of heavy metal with a removable man, made of chrome, to drive it. Shortly after Christmas Dellon removed the driver and buried him among the greasewood bushes behind our houses. Try as we might we could not get him to show us where he buried the man or to retrieve the toy himself. He would only say, "The tractor fell back and killed him and you don't dig up dead people."

Among my gifts that year was one of the By-Lo dolls that were very popular. The realistic little heads were patterned after an infant's head in a maternity hospital. This should have been Dellon's gift because at eleven, I only used dolls to decorate my bed. He confiscated the doll and soon after accidentally bumped its head against the clock. The fragile head cracked in half. Dellon began crying, "Oh, Baby has a headache." I assured him that Baby would be fine, then placed the doll in a box and left it. I didn't want Dellon scolded for the accident, but he gave the secret away himself one day when he asked my mother, "Aunt Vina, will you tell Santa to bring us another baby like the one I broke?"

According to my little red diary I returned to school on January 2, 1928. Miss Mistrot asked me to deliver a note to Mr. Williamson's office, and there I came face to face with my long-lost bosom pal from Santa Rita, Geneva Loyce Smith. Amid squeals and flying books, we hugged each other and danced with glee. Mr. Williamson was astonished, and Mrs. Smith, who had brought her daughter to enroll in school, kept shushing us until we remembered that this was the principal's office.

Miss Mistrot had a new pupil that day, and I was so excited I couldn't sit still until four o'clock when Geneva Loyce and I could really get together. That night my diary read: "January 2, 1928. Today I found my good friend Geneva Loyce Smith in McCamey. I now have a 'reely' truly friend again which I have not had since Jewel Oliver left. I am so happy today."

The early days of 1928 saw an outbreak of scarlet fever in McCamey. Many children were out of school for weeks at a time, but I seemed to be lucky—that is, until Dellon took the dread disease. He was quarantined, and I had to stay away from his house. I was so worried about him that my mother finally let me go to the window beside his bed and wave at him. After that I went by the window after school each afternoon. One unseasonably warm day I went to wave at him and found the window open. Aunt Ira was in the back hanging clothes on the line, and when I turned to go Dellon put his lips next to the screen and requested,

"Gimme kiss." I kissed him through the screen, but the screen was no barrier to scarlet fever germs. Nine days later I got sick at school.

Miss Mistrot recognized my symptoms and sent me home early. As I walked those few blocks the sky seemed to be turning black. Behind me smoke billowed high and flames licked skyward. The fire seemed to be coming after me, and I ran as fast as I could until I reached our front step. I could go no farther. As Mother and Aunt Ira lifted me onto my cot I heard them discussing the refinery that was burning just northwest of town. There had been an explosion, and they were wondering how many men had been killed.

The fever had my head whirling and my thoughts confused. For several days and nights as my fever soared, I clung to my cot and cried out, "Get me out of the fire—the fire is coming after me."

We later learned that the fire took the lives of several men. After each such disaster my parents talked of leaving the hazardous oil fields, but their savings accumulated so slowly they were unable to make the leap from their small measure of security into the unknown.

Dellon was not recovering from scarlet fever as rapidly as I did. He seemed nervous and listless. The doctor suggested that goat milk might be good for him, so Uncle Buss bought a little brown nanny goat, and Dellon named her Brownie.

Brownie was more like a mischievous puppy than a barnyard animal. She ate shoes, belts, toys and organdy collars from dresses hung on the line. She followed at the heels of anyone who went outside and tried to force her way into the house or cars. She even climbed atop the tractor and expected a ride. Dellon and I loved her and encouraged her antics, but Uncle Buss called her "damn goat" and Aunt Ira chased her out of the house with the broom.

One Sunday Aunt Ira, Mother, Dellon and I had gone to Sunday school and church at the Baptist Church. As the hymn of invitation was ending the service, we heard the "rat-tat-tat" of tiny hooves in the front entrance and a definite "Baaaa—" at the door. Dellon's eyes sparkled as he whispered, "Brownie!" Aunt Ira shot out of her seat and down the aisle, with the three of us close behind. My poor embarrassed aunt, dressed in her Sunday best, had to drag that reluctant goat all the way home, with Brownie bleating and digging her sharp little hooves into the crusty earth with every step. I tried to help by pushing the goat from behind while my mother sought to comfort Dellon, whose cries were drowning out the bleating of the goat. He thought the rope was hurting Brownie's neck. When Uncle Buss, in his backyard, caught sight of this procession, he held his sides and laughed. But when Aunt Ira said, "Get a chain for this goat," he lost no time in finding a chain. Nobody made a rope too tough for those sharp little teeth.

With the scarlet fever epidemic over, my life became routine. I took lessons in "Expression" twice a week and played with Geneva Loyce every day. We read *Pollyanna* and *Rebecca of Sunnybrook Farm* at least ten times each and memorized every movie magazine we could get our hands on. We dressed ourselves in our mothers' clothes and borrowed their cosmetics to play Colleen Moore and Constance Bennett. We learned to do a high-kicking dance to the music of "Hand Me down My Walking Cane" played on the Smiths' Victrola.

At school we played with the girls and chased the boys, or ran from them at the slightest provocation. If we found ourselves in danger of being caught by one of the boys we headed for the girls' outhouse, where the boys dared not go. We often discussed the fact that this was a little unfair, since the boys never took refuge in their own outhouse. On the other hand, the boys could run faster and were never in danger of being caught.

We studied our lessons together and, at times, studied our

faces in the mirror, deciding we were hopeless. With Geneva's heavy horn-rimmed glasses and my crooked teeth we could never be movie stars. Geneva Loyce would settle for being a secretary, and I would be a teacher. Then there were times when we reverted to the childhood we had never fully left behind and rode stick horses and played Tom Mix with Dellon. Or we would be very ladylike and babysit with Geneva Loyce's baby sister, Edith Rae.

Around March first, when the spring sandstorms began to darken the sky, the Bumgardners moved to a new oil field at Wink, Texas. I knew that these happy days were numbered, for wherever the Bumgardners went we were sure to follow.

On April 22 I had to give up the McCamey school, Miss Mistrot, the "Expression" lessons that I loved and, worst of all, Geneva Loyce, the bosom pal I had found for the second time. I feared that I would never be lucky enough to find her again.

Wink, Texas
1928

GIANT DUNES OF SUGAR-FINE SAND glowing pinkish in the sun greeted us in Winkler Country. There was an oil well behind almost every dune. The town of Wink had grown from a few oil shacks gathered around the discovery well of the Hedrick Pool, but our reason for being there was not oil. It was water. The clear, cool water flowing from beneath this miniature Sahara was more priceless than oil.

Special machinery used high pressure gas to literally blow the water from wells that were three hundred feet deep. The water was stored in tanks and piped out for use by the oil company. My father's job was to keep that machinery operating.

This was the easiest job my father ever had. He located our tent-cabin within easy walking distance of the pumping operation and was able to spend more time at home than ever before. But we still had a problem.

We were several miles outside the wide open boomtown of Wink, and there was no place for me to go to school. I did not want to miss the last six weeks of the sixth grade, so we finally made arrangements for me to go to Fort Worth and live with Aunt Lela until the term ended and possibly for six weeks of the summer term.

The Bumgardners were planning a trip to Corpus Christi to visit Aunt Ira's family, so they offered to take me to Fort Worth. I was excited about staying with the Bakers and attending a big city school. We packed my best clothes, and I set out on my first venture away from home.

The discovery well of the Wink field. This was a wildcat venture that paid off. Paul Frame Scrapbook Collection. Courtesy the Petroleum Museum, Midland, Texas.

My uncle was driving an open touring car, and once we had passed Big Lake rain began to fall. It rained torrents. The tourist cabins we rented leaked like the toolshed my father and I had lived in back in Santa Rita. We were a wet, tired and bedraggled bunch when we reached the Bakers' house in Fort Worth.

Fort Worth
1928

THE LIGHT-STUDDED DOME of the Tarrant County Court-house reminded me of a princess. When Uncle Sam took us all out for ice cream cones in the evening, Vivian and I tried to count the lights or jewels in her crown.

It was nice but different living at the Bakers' house with its many rooms. The living room was crowded with overstuffed furniture, and there were wool rugs on all the floors except the kitchen and bath. The bathroom was inside the house and had a huge white bathtub that could hold four kids at a time. Aunt Lela and Uncle Sam drove identical Nash automobiles, and I loved to see those cars gleaming in the garage each night.

Uncle Sam, along with his father and brothers, was a contractor of brick work. He wore heavy shoes and overalls for laying brick, but in the evenings and on weekends he wore dress clothes, usually a dark suit, white shirt and tie. His shoes were always black and highly polished. I was impressed, because my father wore a suit only to church or to funerals.

I walked to school each morning with Vivian and Bill. Louise wanted to go with us but was a little too young. Juanita, a golden haired two-year-old, toddled after us as we played each afternoon after school. We treated her like a toy, pushing her in the doll buggy or trundling her up and down the sidewalks in Bill's little red wagon. I thought it would be nice if I had this many brothers and sisters to play with at home.

Quite often in the evenings Aunt Lela took us on picnics to the Lake Worth Amusement Park while Uncle Sam attended the baseball games. He was an avid fan of the Fort Worth Cats. I loved to go to the amusement park, especially when we parked near the open-air pavilion where couples twirled on a dance floor that extended out over the waters of the lake. I loved watching the colored lights sparkle on the water and the ladies dancing in their evening gowns. I once asked Aunt Lela, "Can you tell which is a flapper and which a vamp?" She laughed and answered, "Gosh, no. You ask the darndest questions."

I enjoyed almost everything about Fort Worth except the offensive odor that came from the vast stockyards area when the wind came from that direction. Fort Worth was famous for its stockyards and meat-packing plants. Living there seemed nicer and easier than life in the oil fields. If only my parents were with me, I would have become sold on city life. Attending school in the city, however, was traumatic.

From the day I entered the elementary school in the Bakers' neighborhood, I felt thoroughly intimidated. In changing from class to class, I often became helplessly lost. Once I committed the unpardonable sin of walking down a stairway that was designated for going up only. The hall teacher blew a shrill whistle and shrieked at me, "You know better than to walk down those stairs! Now go back up and come down the others!" I'm sure she wasn't aware that I was a new student, but I was careful never to walk near her again.

The girls in my class all seemed to have lily-white skin and long blonde curls. What's more, they dressed in frocks I considered nice enough for Sunday School. I was painfully aware of my sun-browned skin and dark hair, streaked by the West Texas sun. The once-lovely dresses Mother had made for me now seemed homely and sadly out of style. My self-confidence and ability to make friends deserted me. During my six weeks there I was never able to form a friendship with another girl, either in the classroom or on the playground.

Having never coped with a school lunchroom, I lived in fear of losing my lunch money. I tied it into the corner of a handkerchief and looped it through my belt or pinned it inside my pocket. One morning at recess I stood in the playground line until it was finally my turn to swing. Afraid I might lose my handkerchief as I swung my allotted ten times, I asked the classmate behind me in line to hold it for me since she would be swinging next. When my turn was over the girl was gone and so was my money.

Nobody seemed to notice that I merely sat in the lunchroom while the others ate lunch. I went to my homeroom teacher and reported what had happened. She questioned the guilty girl privately, then turned to me, "You are mistaken," she said. "She didn't take your money. You probably just dropped it somewhere." She turned away, and that was that.

Some of my subjects gave me trouble too. I made A in reading, spelling, language and geography, but arithmetic was my nemesis, even though my math teacher was quite understanding and gave me all the help she could in the short time left in the term.

Art, music and especially penmanship also found me unmistakably six years behind the class. I had never attended a class in public school music, the few oil painting lessons Mrs. Arrington had given us back in Santa Rita did not prepare me for public school art, and all the writing lessons I had ever had were with pencil until the first day I attended Miss Pumphrey's class. I could no more control that pen staff than I could sprout wings and fly back to Wink which, given the chance, I would gladly have done.

Miss Pumphrey counted and clapped her hands. "Ovals, one, two, three, four," and "Push-pulls, one, two, three, four, five and swing." The pen stabbed holes in my paper and dropped blobs of ink everywhere. Ink was dripping from my right wrist when the lesson ended. When the teacher came to collect my paper, she held it gingerly, by one corner, making sure it did not touch the other papers. As she neared her desk, another teacher entered the room and cast a quizzical look at the messy paper. Miss Pumphrey held it out for her to see, and, though she whispered, I saw her lips form the words, "oil field child."

I didn't hear another word through the remainder of the period and the study period that followed. My anger mounted by the minute, and as soon as the last bell sounded, I rushed out of the building and down the center of the boulevard toward my aunt's house. Tears, choked back during the study period, poured down my face and spilled on the stack of books I carried. I could not go home crying, so I sat under one of the trees that marched in a straight line down the grassy center of the boulevard, leaned against the tree trunk and let the tears flow.

"I hate that old woman," I told myself. "I hate this school and all the teachers and students." As school children passed by me I was careful to keep my head turned away from them. Finally they were all gone, and I was alone in my misery.

If I could not learn penmanship, I reasoned, I could never be a teacher. I might as well have stayed in the Winkler County sand-hills and failed the sixth grade. I was going to fail anyway, because I couldn't read music, draw pictures or make push-pulls!

Aunt Lela would begin to worry about me soon, so I began gathering the books I had dropped beside me. On top of the stack was the thin, red booklet Miss Pumphrey had given me that day. Its title was *Palmer Method*. I flipped it open to the first page.

There, pictured in detail, were all the instructions. How to sit, how to hold the pen, how to let your arm glide on its muscle. Slowly I flipped the pages. "By golly, I can learn to do this all by myself," I said aloud. Then another thought struck me. Maybe there were books on art and music that would teach me what I had missed. If so, I had to find them!

My heels struck the sidewalk like jackhammers as I hurried home, dry-eyed now but muttering to myself, "I'll show you, mean old Miss Pumphrey. I'll make better push-pulls than you ever made! I'll be a better teacher than you are too. I'm going to love every one of my students, and I'll never, never, NEVER call a child an oil field child." I had to think about that for a while. I am an oil field child, I admitted. Then why do I care if I'm called one? Is it because I want to prove that an oil field child is just as good as any other child? Yes, I'm sure that is what I want to do. But how can I do it?

My cousin Vivian was already quite good at penmanship. We practiced together, and I finally began to get a feel for the pen. Her art workbook taught me the primary and binary colors and the basic shapes. I got other books from the public library and not only learned more about art but discovered the treasure trove that a big public library can be. I had never seen so many books in one place, and I wondered if a person could ever read all of them. Within a few weeks I had a rough idea of what art was all about. That left public school music, and that's where Frank came to my rescue.

Frank lived next door to the Bakers. He was in another section of the sixth grade and quite a good student. He taught me about lines, spaces, notes and clef signs, and I struggled to memorize as much as I could. He also helped me with arithmetic homework and seemed to have an uncanny knowledge of what to expect on a test.

The adults in both families teased Frank and me about being sweethearts. We were too timid to deny it, and our so-called courtship extended to homework, roller skating on the front sidewalk, and an occasional Saturday afternoon movie along with my three cousins and Frank's brother. On these occasions the girls sat in lower floor seats while the boys chose the balcony. The only romance we were interested in was between the cowboy actor and his horse.

Frank and I discussed these things once, as we were buckling on our skates. He asked me, "Does it embarrass you when they call us sweethearts?"

"Yes," I admitted. "Doesn't it embarrass you?"

"Sure, but do you think we are?" he asked.

"I don't think so. What do you think?"

"I think . . . " he studied for a moment, "I think you are my friend and you are a girl, and I am your friend who happens to be a boy."

"That's exactly right," I agreed, "so next time they tease us, why don't you tell them that?"

"Aw, I don't wanna tell them anything," he said, and we both skated off down the sidewalk.

I felt so insecure about my progress in the fine arts subjects that I was almost sure of being retained in the sixth grade. My parents and Aunt Lela evidently thought so too, for arrangements were made between Mother and Aunt Lela for me to remain with her through the first term of summer school. I agreed to this, though I was already having bouts of homesickness that made me physically ill. The days were fine, but when night came I thought only of my parents, sitting under the canopy in front of our tent, watching the moon rise over the sugar-white sandhills. I could almost feel the desert coolness that would move in as soon as the sun had dropped behind the western dunes. The stars would be appearing, one by one, as the blue sky turned to black, lit here and there by gas torches, like giant candles in the night. This feeling was akin to the loneliness I felt when my mother was away at the sanitorium, but I had my father to help me then.

With the pressure of the coming final exams I had more and more trouble keeping my homesickness confined to the night hours. I did not even realize that my extra study efforts were beginning to pay off in small ways. Penmanship was first.

At the end of my fifth week Miss Pumphrey remarked, as she

stacked my paper with the others, "You have made a lot of progress since you've been in this class."

I looked into her eyes as I answered, but I did not smile. "Thank you. I practice a lot at home." I didn't want her taking credit for my improvement though, inadvertently, she probably was responsible. She made me mad enough to do it myself.

I had finally reached a barely acceptable level in arithmetic, if I could only retain it through the final exam. I figured with music and art, it would be a toss-up whether I passed or not. The weekend before finals I became so desperate that I wrote the letter I had wanted to write for weeks:

> *Dearest Mother and Daddy,*
>
> *I cannot stay here for summer school, even if I do fail. I want to come home, but I don't want to hurt Aunt Lela's feelings because she is so good to me.*
>
> *Please write me a letter and tell me to come home. Send money too. I love you both.*
>
> *Estha*

With the letter in the mail I went to my tests more calm than I had been in weeks. I would do the best I could, but I was not going to worry about it. I would be going home regardless of the outcome of the tests, and that was all that concerned me.

I made good grades on reading, spelling, geography and English and squeaked by on arithmetic, penmanship and music. Only the art test remained. I studied the art basics for hours the night before; I had to rely on my ability to memorize.

To my surprise there was only one question on the test: What is your favorite animal? Answer with a water-color drawing.

We were issued large sheets of manila paper and given an hour to make our drawings. I decided to draw a cow, but I got its neck too long so I decided to make a giraffe out of it. Then I drew trees and vines all around it, like Mrs. Arrington had taught us to do in landscapes. It was a terrible drawing and in no way fit the description of art, but it got me a grade of Satisfactory. I was never so proud of a barely passing grade. I was not retained in the sixth grade, but my report card suggested that I do some remedial work in summer school. I might do that somewhere, I thought, but not here.

A letter from Mother came by return mail along with a money order for more than enough to pay my train fare. I'm sure Mother wrote Aunt Lela later and explained what happened, but I was saved from explaining.

The entire Baker family saw me off on the Texas and Pacific passenger train at 5:30 A.M. on that happy June morning. I clutched the little red purse containing my ticket and spending money. Aunt Lela had sewed a little cloth bag for my extra money, which she pinned inside my dress. I was to unpin it only in a dire emergency.

The train rumbled west all through the day. I ate the lunch Aunt Lela had packed for me and bought candy and soda pop from vendors who padded up and down the aisles, hawking their wares. I passed a lot of time playing with a baby whose mother had taken the seat facing me. By afternoon the grass and trees had disappeared, and we were crossing the flat prairies of West Texas. When I began seeing oil derricks out the window I knew I was nearing home. The sun was down when the conductor called out, "Pyote, all out for Pyote." That was my station.

I was the happiest girl in Texas when I jumped from the high steps of the passenger car to hug my parents. We loaded my suitcases in the Overland, drove twenty-five miles to Wink, and took the sandy lease road through the dunes until we reached our tent. It looked like a palace to me.

John Howard Payne must have said it best: Be it ever so humble, there's no place like home.

Winkler County Sandhills
1928

LIVING IN THE SANDHILLS in July was like living in Dante's Inferno. By midday the sand got too hot for me to walk the short distance to the Bumgardners' tent. All the men wore hightop boots to keep the hot sand from pouring into their shoes. When we went outside we wore straw hats and long sleeves to protect our skin from the blistering rays. Even with these precautions our skin became much darker from reflected rays of the sun.

My father put a fly over our tent to make it cooler. The fly was an additional canvas installed several inches above the tent top, shading the top and leaving room for an air passage between the two layers of canvas.

The sides of our tent-cabin were, as always, screened above the four-foot high walls, and we kept the tent flaps rolled high, inviting the daytime breezes. As the sun dropped, so did the temperature, and the nights were cool enough to require a light blanket for sleeping.

Almost all our work was done in the early morning and late evening. Mother and I rose early each washday in order to have our clothes on the line shortly after sunrise. A short time in the early morning sun dried them just right, but a longer time in the sun made them bone-hard and faded the colors.

Sheets sparkled white when dried in this sunlight, except for the times a wildcat well spewed over the derrick top. Droplets of oil could be carried for miles on the wind, giving our sparkling

The man on the left is Word (Tex) Thornton, whose expertise in fighting oil well fires has been passed through several generations to those men in the business today. Ford Chapman Collection. Courtesy the Petroleum Museum, Midland, Texas.

sheets ugly brown polka dots that could be removed only by boiling them in soapy water.

Wells were being drilled all over these sandhills, most of them wildcats or wells drilled at random in unproven territory without benefit of geological data. Each well that blew in was an exciting event. Crowds often gathered when a driller was thought to be nearing "pay dirt," just to see the excitement as the ground rumbled and a black stream rose higher and higher until it finally flowed over the derrick and fell in a high arc to the ground. It drenched the area for miles around until the flow was brought under control by setting a "Christmas tree," the giant fitting that controlled the flow, sending it down pipe lines and into huge storage tanks.

A typical wildcat drilling rig of the type used when relatively shallow production was expected. On display at the Petroleum Museum, Midland, Texas. Photo by Dick Stowe.

Oil from the Winkler pool was accompanied by gas, and the greatest danger was igniting the gas with a spark. An oil well fire was spectacular and exciting but very dangerous and expensive. One well in the sandhills burned for days, roaring bright orange by day and lighting up the nights with a blinding brightness. All efforts to extinguish it were in vain until Tex Thornton arrived by plane.

My uncle got word that the famous oil-fire fighter had been called in, so we drove to an open area where the rig was visible though still more than a mile away. We parked along with other viewers and sat in the car to watch the activity as trucks, tractors, draglines and men busied themselves like ants in the terrific heat near the well. The roar was deafening, even that far away.

"How is he going to get close enough to put the nitroglycerine in?" Dellon shouted to his father.

"He's wearing an asbestos suit," my uncle answered.

It seemed like hours of milling around, moving machinery and changing men's positions before the word went out, "Now!" We glued our eyes on the inferno, and suddenly there was a thunderous report. The fire seemed to rip loose from its moorings and leap toward the sky, then the earth went black. Our eyes, accustomed to the glare, struggled to adjust to the total darkness. The roar had stopped and only a hissing sound was heard. It was all over, and people began turning on car lights, searching for a way to leave the scene.

"Boy, he is really brave," Dellon said.

"He's a daredevil," said my mother.

Tex Thornton, hero of the hour, was the topic of conversation as we drove home to take baths and get a full night's sleep with only stars to light the sky.

Our desert camp lacked many amenities but, happily, bathwater was plentiful. We could use all we wanted and did not pay the customary one dollar per barrel for it. My father built a wooden sled, capable of holding two barrels. We pulled the sled behind the car the short distance to the water wells and back. The front barrel on the sled was always parked under the canopy in front of the tent to keep it cool, while the back barrel was left in the sun all day. By night we had just enough warm water to use in our washtub baths.

This forerunner of the solar water heating system was a great help. Our cooking was done on a kerosene range, and the tent was lighted with two huge Dad's Lanterns, one hung in each end of the tent. A Dad's Lantern used two large dry cell batteries like those used in early day telephones. They were carried by a bucket-style bail and were usually bright red. We used the lanterns sparingly to make the batteries last longer. A large fire extinguisher hung just inside the tent door, for my parents were very cautious about the possibility of fire.

The sandhill road leading out to the highway was bladed daily, then oiled or watered to keep the sand firm enough to support a car. The best time to travel this road was just after the grader and water truck had finished their work.

Mother made a trip to town for groceries at least once a week. The night after one of these trips we always had iced tea, for Mother brought back twenty-five pounds of ice. It never lasted over twelve hours. I usually accompanied Mother on these trips to Wink, and she often took me to the drugstore and let me choose magazines to read. I liked them all but usually bought *Woman's Home Companion* and *Delineator* as well as *Child Life* and puzzle books. Mother never let me buy *True Story* or *True Confessions*. I made no objection to this rule because a neighbor woman in a tent near us bought all the current love story magazines and stacked the ones she had read in a box behind her tent. I read them all and wondered what was supposed to be so shocking about the stories, but I didn't ask.

There were only two other children in camp, Dellon and a

baby girl named Emmalie. I played with them part of the time and practiced penmanship every day. Dellon liked to get a pencil and paper and practice with me. One day Uncle Buss came in as we practiced a line of A, B, C to my rhythmical count.

"My gosh," he remarked, "she's teaching him Palmer Method before he goes to kindergarten."

I did anything to keep busy, but I was restless and needed the company of someone my age. In addition, I felt I was a problem to my parents. They worried about the coming school term and the fact that their savings were still less than sufficient for the little business Daddy dreamed of having. They had been able to save a good bit since they had been on this job and a few more months would do the trick. But September was not even a month away.

I felt guilty for leaving Fort Worth, yet I was constantly afraid they would decide to send me back. I did not want to stay away from home, but I did want to go to school. Luckily, fate intervened this time.

Mother came home from Wink one day bringing a letter that had been forwarded so many times it was hard to tell where it originated. It contained a check for one hundred fifty dollars from one of the families who had lost their belongings in the flood near Crane. My father's eyes filled with tears, but he smiled as he held up the check.

"That's the last of the money I loaned," he said, "and I didn't lose a dime."

Mother was touched, too. "This is proof," she said, "that it never hurts to help your fellow man."

The check put their savings a trifle over the goal they had set, so my father began writing letters, trying to get a line on a small grocery store he could purchase. By the first of August he had letters concerning several possibilities, so he sold our tent to the man who took the water pumper's job, loaded our belongings on a small trailer and headed east.

Before we were out of the sandhills a Caterpillar tractor driver fell asleep at his controls and hit our trailer, knocking it loose from the car, overturning it and scattering our belongings over the blistering sand.

Daddy and the driver repaired the trailer hitch and began trying to reload it. Mother's pride and joy, the white enamel kerosene range, was smashed beyond repair. She looked at the far horizon to choke back tears as the men stacked it beside the road.

Suddenly from a small cloud no bigger than a bedspread there came a torrent of rain. We worked frantically jamming clothes and bedding into the car to keep them from being soaked. We were soon drenched to the skin and our mattresses and pillows still lay helter-skelter on the sand, soaking wet.

With the rain dripping off his ears and his hair plastered to his head, my father sat down on a wet mattress. He took out a red tobacco can and a package of cigarette papers. The rain had stopped as suddenly as it began, and now the sun was shining. Daddy rolled a cigarette and lighted it. He took a puff, blew out the smoke and began laughing. He laughed louder and louder.

Mother, as wet as the rest of us, looked at him as if he had lost his senses. "What on earth is wrong with you, John?" she asked. He couldn't answer, so he shrugged his shoulders and threw out his hands to indicate the whole ridiculous scene.

Mother held an armload of wet clothes, but a mischievous smile crept across her face. She stepped over to my father, shoved him backward on the wet mattress and piled the wet clothing on top of him. Her long hair had escaped from its pins and tumbled in dripping strands about her shoulders. She sat down on the mattress and laughed until she cried. By this time I was laughing, not so much at the situation as at my parents, but the tractor driver, who had caused the whole thing, could only manage a sort of quizzical grin.

We stacked the wet bedding beside the road along with our

wrecked stove, and our load was much smaller when we were on the road again. But that little rain cloud must have been a bad omen for us. Before out trip ended, the car broke down three times, and all four tires had to be replaced with new ones.

Our first stopover was in Big Spring where my father spent three days looking into a deal for a grocery store, only to decide against it. We made inquiries in several other towns along the way but found nothing to his liking. Our last contact was to be made in Mineral Wells, where he had heard of a grocery store and filling station for sale. We really hoped this one would work out. Mother and I liked Mineral Wells because it had mountains, like Mc-Camey. Daddy could not work out a deal, so we passed it up.

"What shall we do now?" Mother asked.

"Let's go out to Graford and visit Arthur and Cora. Maybe he can put me on to a store for sale in one of these small towns."

This Arthur we were about to visit was my father's older brother, the one who, several years earlier, sat under our table in Mexia to put on his shoes. He was a partner in the Model Grocery at Graford now, and his new wife had left a career in the county offices of Jack County to marry him.

We turned the little Overland toward Graford, eighteen miles northwest of Mineral Wells, in Palo Pinto County. The town lay in a valley between Keechi Creek and the Brazos River, surrounded by farms and ranches with a range of hills not far to the west. Large, lacy mesquite trees grew along the roadside while tall elm, oak, and native pecan trees lined the banks of Keechi Creek where a wood-floored bridge crossed the stream just east of town.

The town was small and each family seemed to have a garden plot and space for a cow and chickens. As we drove into town, Mother said, "What a homey looking town!" And that is what it became—our hometown.

My father established his grocery store and later a small truck line. Mother found a permanent home at last, and though she missed the high, dry climate of the west, she was quite content, especially after Uncle Buss, Aunt Ira and Dellon joined us in Graford. And it was only a two-hour drive to Aunt Lela's house in Fort Worth.

But I was happiest of all, for I had a hometown to call my own, a school to attend year after year, and a crowd of friends to keep forever.

My parents in 1937.

Epilogue: Odessa
1937

IN AUGUST 1937 I worked as a cashier in the Lyric Drug Store in Odessa. This was a working vacation for me as I was spending a few weeks with my parents before time to report for my first teaching assignment at Progress School near Mineral Wells on September 15.

A year earlier, while I was busy at East Texas State Teachers College in Commerce, working to complete my teaching require- ments, my parents had heard the siren song of the latest oil boom in the Permian Basin and moved to Odessa.

W. B. Looney, my father's brother-in-law and for many years a road construction contractor, had taken a contract for moving road materials in the Odessa area and needed additional trucks and drivers which my father was happy to supply.

The Looney family, including W. B. and Loice, who was my father's sister, their daughter and son-in-law, Edna and P. J. How- ten, another daughter, Billie Mae Bridges and her small son Bill, were already in Odessa when my parents arrived. The six weeks I spent there gave me an opportunity to become acquainted with these relatives whom I had known only slightly before. I had no trouble finding a job and fitting into this affable group.

The Lyric was a small soda fountain-tobacco counter opera- tion tucked into the side of the Lyric Theater, directly across from the Elliot Hotel. From my cash register, just inside a plate glass window, I watched the life of yet another oil town go by and, oh! how different it was from the boomtowns of my childhood.

Odessa had no axle-deep mud, no wooden store fronts or resounding boardwalks. Permanent buildings lined paved streets and sidewalks. Gone, too, were the horse-drawn wagons and Model T trucks, replaced by huge, portable well-servicing trucks and smart pickups bearing colorful company logos.

Odessa and her sister city, Midland, formed the hub of the giant Permian Basin, then called the richest deposit of oil in the world. For miles around the two cities, life moved at an exciting pace.

Rotary drills with fast-turning bits now cut through dirt and rock to drill the wells, replacing the old cable tool rigs that beat their way into the earth like giant butter churns. There were no more boilers, belthouses or bull wheels. Neat white seismograph trucks took the place of human oil witchers with their peeled willow limbs or divining rods for finding oil beneath the earth. Wildcat drillers no longer had to risk their fortunes punching holes at random, hoping to discover the needle-in-a-haystack pool of oil.

Midland and Odessa sprouted modern homes, schools, churches and municipal buildings as if they had no fear of becoming ghost towns when the boom was over. All this progress labeled me a pioneer in the oil patch, and I was barely old enough to vote.

I was glad my parents had returned to West Texas, the land they loved best. And it was a special thrill for me, at the threshold of my own career, to feel the throb and beat of black gold fever one more time, for I knew Odessa would be my last oil boomtown.

At the age of twenty-one I was
ready to begin a teaching career.

Acknowledgements

Thanks for facts about your cities, past and present,
    Crane County Chamber of Commerce, Crane, Texas
    Kermit Chamber of Commerce, Kermit, Texas
        Mr. Lindsey J. Rhodes
    McCamey Chamber of Commerce, McCamey, Texas
        Mrs. Peggy Garner
    Mexia Chamber of Commerce, Mexia, Texas
        Mr. J. C. Killingsworth
Thanks for inspiration,
    The Western Company Museum, Ft. Worth, Texas
    The East Texas Oil Museum, Kilgore, Texas
    The Petroleum Museum, Midland, Texas
    Mr. C. K. Stillwagon, author of *Rope Chokers*
Thanks for information and photographs,
    Mrs. Betty Orbeck and Mrs. Martha Hunt
    Archivists, The Petroleum Museum, Midland, Texas
Thanks for gathering family information,
    Mrs. Madge L. Quate
Thanks for saying, "Write that down", Winnie Reeser.
Thanks for sharing your memories,
    Dellon E. Bumgardner Lt. Col. USAF Reserve, Ret.
Thanks for typing the manuscript, Velma Yount.
Thanks also to my parents, Vina and John Briscoe (now deceased)
    for telling me their life story in the sixty-fourth year of their
    marriage.

About the Author

ESTHA B. STOWE completed this, her first book, just before her seventy-second birthday. She was born at Waldrip, McCullough County, Texas and spent her childhood in the early-day oil fields. She claims the distinction of having played in the shadow of the wooden derrick on the Santa Rita No. 1, the well that made millions of dollars for the University of Texas and heralded the discovery of Texas' famous Permian Basin oil fields.

Mrs. Stowe received her education at Hardin-Simmons University in Abilene and East Texas State Teachers College (now E.T.S.U.) in Commerce. She went on to become a teacher, wife, mother, traveler and free-lance writer. Her articles have appeared in Texas newspapers and national magazines. She is the author of a historical drama/pageant which brought to life the history of Irving, Texas, on the city's fiftieth anniversary. She and her husband of forty-nine years are parents of one son and make their home in Irving but spend much time traveling.